Why He'll Never Choose You

The Raw Truth About Being His Option, Not His Priority, and How to Break the Pattern for Good

TABLE OF CONTENTS

INTRODUCTION

THE SCIENCE OF BEING SECOND BEST

You stare at the glowing screen. The silence in the room is overwhelming. You wait for a text that may never come. You wonder why you are always the one checking the clock. This is not just a bad night. It is a biological event. Your brain processes this silence as a physical injury.

When you feel like an option, your body reacts with alarm. Magnetic resonance imaging (MRI) shows that social rejection activates the dorsal anterior cingulate cortex (dACC). This is the same part of the brain that handles physical pain. Heartbreak is not a metaphor. It is a neurological reality. Your brain does not know the difference between a broken heart and a broken bone.

Why does this happen?. Your brain evolved to treat social bonds as survival tools. For our ancestors, being pushed to the edge of the group meant death. Rejection acts as a biological alarm system to alert you that your welfare is in danger. In the current world, this alarm goes off when he leaves you on "read" for three days. It goes off when he makes last-minute plans only when he is bored. Your nervous system is trying to protect you.

This book looks at the raw truth of these patterns. We look at the facts of why you get stuck in the "option" cycle. You will learn how to shift from being a backup plan to being your own priority.

The Addictive Cycle of the "Maybe"

Being an option creates a specific type of chemical hook. This is often called a trauma bond. It is built through cycles of coldness followed by small bursts of warmth. Psychologists call this intermittent reinforcement. It is the same mechanism that makes slot machines addictive.

When he finally texts after a week of silence, your brain gets a surge of dopamine. This surge is much stronger than if he were consistent. Your brain learns that uncertain rewards are more valuable than guaranteed ones. You become addicted to the "high" of his occasional attention. This chemical storm makes you feel like you are in love, but you are actually experiencing withdrawal.

Leaving a relationship like this feels like quitting a drug cold turkey. You experience cravings, anxiety, and even physical pain. You might obsessively check his social media to get a "fix" of connection. This is your reward system trying to correct an error. It wants the dopamine back. To break the pattern, you must see this for what it is: a chemical trap.

The Stress of Living on Standby

Chronic uncertainty is a form of emotional abuse. It keeps your body in a state of high alert. Your amygdala scans for danger constantly. This triggers the release of cortisol and norepinephrine. Cortisol increases your heart rate and blood pressure. If these levels stay high, they can harm your immune system.

You might feel jumpy, tired, or unable to focus. You walk on eggshells to avoid distance or criticism. You start to blame yourself for his mood swings. This stress erodes your self-esteem. You begin to believe you are unworthy of respect outside of this bond.

How do we stop this erosion? It starts with self-awareness. You must identify the moments where you feel drained or resentful. These feelings are data. They tell you that a value is being stepped on. You must learn to name your emotions to engage your prefrontal cortex. This part of your brain helps you regulate feelings and make logical choices.

Reclaiming Your Relational Value

Your brain maintains an internal model of how much others value you. This is your "relational value". When you accept being an option, you recalibrate your perceived worth downward. You start to think that "crumbs" are all you deserve.

This book provides the tools to update that internal model. We use techniques from Dialectical Behavior Therapy (DBT) and Cognitive Behavioral Therapy (CBT). You will learn how to set limits that protect your peace. You will learn to use "I" statements to express your needs clearly.

Key Shift	From Option Mindset	To Priority Mindset
Communication	Waiting for permission to speak	Direct and assertive
Boundaries	Blurred and non-existent	Clear lines with consequences
Worth	Based on his validation	Internal and self-defined
Action	Reactive and anxious	Proactive and calm

The Road to Priority

Healing is a journey of reclaiming your power. You must acknowledge the reality of what happened without blame. You are not "foolish" for catching feelings for an unavailable person. Your brain followed a familiar template from your past.

The chapters ahead will guide you through this process. We will look at how to recognize digital mind games. We will look at how to trust your body to sense danger. You will learn how to build a life that you love alone so that you never settle again.

You have the capacity for neuroplasticity. This means your brain can learn new ways of thinking and being. You can rewire your response to stress. You can rebuild your sense of self step by step.

Stop waiting for a text. Start living for yourself. You stop being an option when you realize you are the prize. It is time to choose yourself today.

Scientific Note on the Anterior Cingulate Cortex (ACC)

The ACC acts as a center for the emotional component of pain. It helps the brain detect gaps between what we expect and what we get. When a partner is inconsistent, the ACC flares up because the reality does not match the hope. This causes intense emotional distress. Learning to calm the ACC through mindfulness and deep breathing is a vital step in recovery.

The Role of Oxytocin in Trauma Bonding

Oxytocin is often called the "bonding hormone". It builds trust and connection. In a toxic relationship, oxytocin can stay high even when you are being mistreated. This creates a desire for reconciliation even if the person is unkind. Connecting with a support system of friends and family can help balance these hormones.

Conclusion

The pain you feel is a signal that your environment is unsafe. By listening to this signal, you gain the power to change your situation. You are about to walk a path that leads away from crumbs and toward a full life. Let's begin.

PART ONE

THE REALITY OF THE CRUMB

CHAPTER 1

STOP CHASING CRUMBS AND START CHOOSING YOURSELF

You sit on your sofa and look at the screen. The light from your phone reflects in your eyes. You have checked the thread twelve times in the last hour. He saw your message at 2:15 p.m. It is now 8:45 p.m. The silence feels like a physical weight on your chest. You wonder if you said something wrong. You wonder if he is busy. Deep down, you know the truth. You are waiting for a crumb of attention. You are living as an option, not a priority.

This chapter looks at the mechanics of this trap. We look at why your brain keeps you stuck in unfulfilling loops. We look at how to stop the cycle of chasing and start the process of choosing yourself. You deserve a full meal, not the dry crusts of someone else's leftover time.

Defining the "Crumb"

In the world of modern dating, people use a tactic called breadcrumbing. This is a form of relational manipulation. The person sends occasional signals of interest to keep you hooked. They have no real intent to commit to you. They might send a "hey stranger" text or like an old photo. These are low-effort actions. They cost the sender nothing but keep you emotionally tethered.

Breadcrumbing is different from ghosting. When someone ghosts you, they vanish. It hurts, but it is a clean break. Breadcrumbing is a slow drain. It gives you just enough hope to stay invested. It creates a cycle of hope and disappointment. Why do you stay in this cycle? The answer lies in your brain chemistry.

The Science of the Hook

Your brain is a prediction machine. It loves patterns. When a reward is consistent, the brain gets used to it. When a reward is unpredictable, the brain goes into overdrive. This is called intermittent reinforcement.

B.F. Skinner proved this in 1956 with his experiments on animals. He found that rewards delivered sporadically are the hardest to stop seeking. Your brain treats his text like a win on a slot machine. You don't know when the next win is coming. This makes you play longer.

When you get that occasional text, your brain releases dopamine. This is the chemical of motivation and craving. It makes you feel a "high." This high is short-lived. It is followed by a crash when he disappears again. You become addicted to the "fix" of his attention.

This cycle activates the same neural pathways as cocaine addiction. You are not "weak" for staying. You are experiencing a biological withdrawal. Your reward system is hijacked. To break free, you must see this as a chemical loop rather than a romantic connection.

The Mental Toll of Being an Option

Living as an option has a high price. Research shows that breadcrumbing correlates with lower life satisfaction. It increases feelings of loneliness and helplessness. The constant uncertainty creates chronic stress. This stress releases cortisol into your system.

High cortisol levels can harm your body. They lead to sleep issues and digestive problems. You might feel jumpy or anxious. You start to walk on eggshells. You blame yourself for his silence. This erodes your self-esteem.

The brain also calculates your "relational value." This is your internal model of how much others value you. When you accept crumbs, your brain recalibrates your worth downward. You start to believe you do not deserve better. This makes you more vulnerable to similar partners in the future.

The Social Exchange Asymmetry

We can look at relationships through Social Exchange Theory. This theory says we seek to maximize rewards and minimize costs.

$$Value = Rewards - Costs$$

For the person breadcrumbing you, the value is high. They get your attention and validation (Reward). They spend almost zero time or energy (Cost). For you, the equation is broken. You spend massive emotional energy and time (Cost). You get rare and vague signals (Reward). Your value is negative.

Why do you accept a negative value? Often, it is because of your attachment style. If you have an anxious attachment style, you interpret inconsistent signals as a sign of potential closeness. You work harder to "fix" the distance, but you cannot fix a person who chooses to stay at a distance to protect their own autonomy.

Transitioning to Self-Priority

Choosing yourself is not a single event. It is a daily practice. It starts with radical honesty. You must look at his actions, not his words. If he says he likes you but never makes plans, trust his lack of action.

The "Let Them" Framework

Mel Robbins introduced a tool called the "Let Them" theory. This is a mindset shift. If he wants to be inconsistent, let him. If he wants to choose other people over you, let him.

You stop trying to manage his behavior. You stop trying to "prove" your worth. When you "let them," you reclaim your energy. You move from an external locus of control to an internal one. You focus on your own response and your own life.

This is not about being passive. It is about emotional independence. You realize that his behavior is about his limitations, not your worth. You detach from the outcome. This reduces your anxiety and stress.

Practical Steps to Stop the Cycle

To break the addiction to crumbs, you need clear rules. You need to build a life that feels good without his validation.

1. **Identify Your Non-Negotiables:** Write a list of what you require in a relationship. Consistency should be at the top. If a person cannot meet these, they are not a match.
2. **Set Time Limits:** If someone reaches out at the last minute, say no. State that you need more notice. This sets a boundary.
3. **Practice Emotional Awareness:** When you feel the urge to check your phone, pause. Ask yourself, "What am I feeling right now?". Is it love or is it anxiety?
4. **Audit Your Support System:** Surround yourself with people who value you consistently. This boosts your oxytocin and reduces the pain of rejection.
5. **Use the FAST Skill:** This is a DBT tool for self-respect. Be Fair to yourself. Stop over-apologizing. Stick to your values. Be Truthful about the reality of the situation.

Reclaiming Your Voice

You must tell people what you need. Clarity is a form of emotional intelligence. If you are looking for a committed relationship, say so early. Do not be afraid to rock the boat. If asking for a plan makes him disappear, let him go.

Dating apps are tools, not validation systems. Your value is not determined by a match or a text. You are the prize. When you stop chasing the crumbs, you make room for someone who wants to give you the whole meal.

You have the power to change your story. Your brain is plastic. You can learn to find peace in your own company. You stop being an option the moment you decide to be your own first priority.

Choosing yourself is a skill. It starts with the truth. You are not a backup plan. You are not a "maybe." Stop waiting for a text that only gives you crumbs. Start living a life that offers you everything you deserve. The path away from the forest is open. Take the first step today.

CHAPTER 2

RECOGNIZE DIGITAL MIND GAMES IN YOUR INBOX

The phone screen glows on your nightstand at 2:00 a.m. You see his name. It is a link to a song or a "like" on a story you posted three days ago. Your heart jumps. You feel a rush of relief. For a second, the anxiety fades. Then, the questions start. Why now? Why this? Why hasn't he asked to see you?

You are caught in a digital web. In our current world, your inbox is the front line for your heart. Technology makes it easy to stay connected. It also makes it easy for him to keep you on a string. These are not accidents. They are digital mind games. They are tools he uses to keep you as an option while he avoids the work of a real priority.

This chapter breaks down the new ways men use screens to manage your feelings. We look at the latest trends from 2025 and 2026. You will learn to spot the tricks before they drain your energy. You will learn how to demand clarity in a world that thrives on being vague.

The Chemistry of the Notification

Your brain is a prediction machine. It works on a simple loop. When you expect a reward and get it, you feel good. When you get a reward you did not expect, you feel even better. This is called a reward prediction error.

Dopamine is the chemical that drives this. It is not about pleasure. It is about the chase. When your phone pings, your brain releases dopamine. You crave the connection. If he is inconsistent, your brain becomes obsessed with the "maybe." Research shows that unpredictable rewards create a stronger hook than steady ones.

This is why you check your phone even when you know he hasn't texted. You are chasing a digital fix. Scans show that this cycle activates the same neural pathways as drug addiction. He is using your own biology against you. He gives you just enough to keep the dopamine flowing, but never enough to make you feel safe.

Identifying New Digital Tricks

As dating changes, so do the tactics. You must know the names of these games to stop playing them. Recent studies from 2025 identify several new behaviors that erode your peace.

Ghostlighting: The Double Hit

Ghostlighting is a mix of ghosting and gaslighting. He vanishes for weeks without a word. When he finally returns, he acts like you are "crazy" for noticed he was gone. He might say you are "too intense" about communication. He disappears and then blames you for the distance. This trick makes you question your own reality. It is a way to avoid accountability for his lack of effort.

Banksying: The Performance Artist

Banksying is when he leaves cryptic signals instead of having a direct talk. He might post a sad quote on his story. He might send a vague song lyric at midnight. He wants you to "get it" without him having to say "I miss you." It is performance art, not emotional honesty. He wants the credit for being deep without doing the work of being present.

Digital Breadcrumbing

This remains the most common trap. He sends low-effort signals like emojis, "likes," or "hey stranger" texts. He wants to see if the door is still open. He wants the ego boost of your reply. He is not building a bridge to you. He is just checking the status of his backup plan.

The "Rejection Mindset" and App Burnout

If you feel exhausted by dating apps, you are not alone. Data from 2025 shows that 79% of Gen Z daters feel "burnt out" by apps. The "illusion of choice" makes everything feel shallow. When you see hundreds of profiles, your brain shifts into a "rejection mindset."

Studies found that as you view more profiles, your chance of accepting a match drops by 27%. You start looking for reasons to say no. You focus on flaws instead of traits. This environment trains you to treat people like items in a shop. It makes it easier for him to view you as one of many options.

This digital fatigue leads to "situationships." These are connections that lack a label or a future. They are built on convenience. In 2026, 70% of users report that digital dating does not align with their actual needs. You are seeking a bond, but the system is built for a scroll.

Trusting the "Seen" Receipt

Digital ambiguity is a choice. In 2026, clarity is the highest form of emotional intelligence. If he leaves you on "read" for days, that is data. It tells you where you sit on his list of priorities.

The human brain processes this type of digital silence as a physical wound. Rejection lights up the dorsal anterior cingulate cortex (dACC). This is the pain center. When he ignores your text, your body feels a literal sting. You might feel a knot in your stomach or a tight chest.

Do not ignore these physical signs. Your body is telling you that this connection is not safe. A person who values you will not leave space for you to doubt your worth. They will provide clear, consistent answers because they want to protect the bond.

Your Digital Protection Plan

You can take back control of your inbox. You do not have to be a victim of his notification schedule. Use these guidelines to reset your digital boundaries.

1. **Turn Off Read Receipts and Notifications:** Stop being a slave to the "ping." Check your messages on your own time. This reduces the dopamine spikes and helps you stay calm.
2. **The "Wait and See" Rule:** When he sends a vague "hey" or a random link, do not rush to reply. Let the message sit. See if he follows up with a real question or a plan. If he doesn't, do not do the work for him.
3. **Clarify Early:** If you are looking for a committed partner, say it. If he says he "doesn't like labels" or "wants to see where it goes" without taking action, believe him. Do not try to win a game that has no prize.
4. **Demand Video or In-Person Dates:** Stop the "nano-ships." These are ultra-short digital bonds that never leave the phone. If he won't get on a video call or meet in person within two weeks, he is a pen pal, not a partner.
5. **Use the "Let Them" Theory:** If he wants to ghost you, let him. If he wants to send cryptic songs, let him. You stop trying to "fix" his behavior. You focus on your own response. You reclaim the energy you wasted on trying to decode his silence.

Living as the Priority

You show people how to treat you by what you accept. If you accept breadcrumbs, you will always be hungry. If you accept ghostlighting, you will always be confused.

A priority partner is consistent. He does not leave you guessing. He integrates you into his life. He makes plans in advance because he values your time. He treats communication as a bridge, not a game of hide-and-seek.

Your inbox should be a source of connection, not a source of stress. The moment you stop chasing his digital crumbs, you free up space for a real meal. You are worth more than a 2:00 a.m. "like." You are the prize. Start acting like it today.

CHAPTER 3

END THE SEARCH FOR SPARSE VALIDATION

You refresh the screen. You look for a tiny red dot or a heart icon. You want a sign that you exist in his thoughts. This hunger for a "like" or a brief compliment is a heavy burden. It feels like a sugar rush. You get a quick spike of joy when he notices you. Then, you crash into doubt when the silence returns. This is the cycle of sparse validation. It keeps you small. It keeps you waiting for someone else to tell you that you matter.

This chapter looks at why we seek approval from people who give us so little. We examine the latest data from 2025 and 2026 on how the brain processes social worth. You will learn to move from a "mattering deficit" to a state of internal security. You will learn how to stop being a consumer of his crumbs and start being the creator of your own value.

The Primal Question: Do I Matter?

Humans are social animals. Our survival once depended on being part of the group. Because of this, the brain evolved a "sociometer." This is an internal gauge that tracks how much others value us. When this gauge is low, we feel social pain.

Researcher Zach Mercurio argues in his 2025 work that the search for significance is the core force of human behavior. He defines "mattering" through three signs: being noticed, being affirmed, and being needed. When you are an option, you lack these three things. He might notice you only when he is bored. He might affirm you only to keep you around. He does not truly need you as an essential part of his life.

This creates a "mattering deficit." You feel invisible. To fix this, you chase "sparse validation." You seek small wins to prove you are still in the game. However, 2025 studies show that external validation from dating apps fosters a dangerous dependence. About 64% of users report that receiving validation motivates them to use apps more often. They adjust their behavior based on random feedback. You start to perform for him instead of being yourself.

The Chemistry of the Validation Trap

Your brain uses two distinct paths to learn about other people. One path tracks "rewarding outcomes," like a fun date or a good text. The second path tracks "relational value." This is your model of how much a partner actually values you.

In a healthy relationship, these two paths align. You get rewards because you have high value. In the "option" cycle, these paths split. Your brain receives a "rewarding outcome" (a text) that does not match your low "relational value" (his lack of effort). This creates a "reward prediction error."

When he finally praises you after weeks of coldness, your dopamine levels spike. This spike is much higher than if he were always kind. Your brain interprets this surprise as a high-value event. You become addicted to the "fix" of his rare approval. You are not seeking love. You are seeking a chemical relief from the anxiety of being ignored.

External vs. Internal Validation

External validation is like a sugar rush. It provides a quick burst of energy but leaves you empty. It relies on factors you cannot control, like his mood or his schedule. If he has a bad day, your self-worth drops. If he forgets to text, you feel worthless.

Internal validation is nourishment. It builds long-term strength. It comes from your own values and actions. You stop asking, "Was I good enough for him?". You start asking, "Was this interaction good enough for me?".

Validation Type	Source	Emotional Result
External	His texts, "likes," and moods	Anxiety and instability
Internal	Your values, goals, and boundaries	Peace and agency

A 2025 study in the *Journal of Affective Disorders* found that how the brain learns from rewards predicts mental health recovery. If you rely on external "hits" of praise, your nervous system stays in a state of alarm. To heal, you must rewire your reward system to value internal metrics.

The Reassurance Compulsion

When you feel like an option, you might find yourself seeking constant reassurance. You ask, "Are we okay?". You check "read receipts" to see if he is ignoring you. You analyze every word of a message for hidden meaning.

In 2026, psychologists identify this as a "reassurance compulsion." It is an emotional habit that reinforces anxiety. Every time you ask for reassurance and get it, you feel a temporary relief. This relief teaches your brain that you cannot handle uncertainty alone. The doubt always comes back stronger.

Breaking this cycle requires "exposure." You must sit with the urge to ask for validation without giving in to it. Start by delaying your response to his name on your screen. Set a timer for ten minutes. Then, move to an hour. Your body will learn that you can survive the silence. This builds your "distress tolerance."

Moving from Performance to Authenticity

Validation-seekers often change their personality to fit in. This is called "Kittenfishing" or "Truecasting" facades. You might pretend to like his hobbies. You might hide your true needs to avoid appearing "intense."

Data from 2025 shows that 70% of people want their dating profiles to be more authentic. People are tired of the performance. When you hide your real self to get his approval, you win a prize that does not fit you. You end up in a "situationship" with a person who does not even know the real you.

A priority mindset requires "Truecasting." This means showing up as your real self from the very first date. You state your values. You share your goals. You do not wait for him to set the tone. If your real self does not get his approval, that is good data. It means he is not your person.

Exercises to Rebuild Internal Security

You can reset your validation loops with specific cognitive drills. These tools help you engage your prefrontal cortex and calm your "social pain network."

1. **The "Thought-on-Trial" Worksheet:** When you feel "not good enough," put that thought on the stand. Write down the evidence for it. Then, write down the evidence against it. Use facts, not feelings. The verdict is usually that your worth is not tied to one person's silence.
2. **The "Mattering" Audit:** Ask yourself three questions today. Did I notice my own needs? Did I affirm my own efforts? Did I do something that I needed for myself? Focus on "Noticed, Affirmed, and Needed" from an internal perspective.
3. **Build "Quiet Wins":** Achieve something meaningful today without telling anyone. Feel the satisfaction of finishing a project or hitting a gym goal. Let the pride sit in your body without needing a "like" to make it real.
4. **The "Let Them" Reset:** If he does not see your value, let him. If he chooses someone else, let him. You stop trying to "prove" your worth to a person who is not looking. You reclaim your energy for your own path.

Living with Significance

You stop being an option when you realize that your significance is not a vote. It is a fact. You do not need a text to confirm that you are a person of value.

When you end the search for sparse validation, you become more attractive to priority partners. Healthy people are drawn to those who have a solid sense of self. They respect those who do not need their constant applause.

Your inbox is just a tool for logistics. Your phone is a device, not a mirror. Put it down. Look at your own life. You are the only person who needs to choose you today. When you provide your own validation, the crumbs from others will no longer interest you. You are ready for the whole meal.

CHAPTER 4

FACE THE REALITY OF ONLINE DATING FATIGUE

You swipe while you wait for your coffee. You swipe while you sit on the bus. You swipe before you close your eyes at night. What started as a fun way to meet people now feels like a second shift at a job you hate. You feel drained, cynical, and bored. You see the same faces and hear the same stale opening lines. This is not just a bad week. It is an epidemic of dating app burnout.

In our current world, technology offers endless access to potential partners. Yet, many women feel more alone than ever. This chapter examines the facts of swipe fatigue. We look at the latest data from 2025 and 2026. You will learn why the apps make you feel like a product on a shelf. You will find the tools to reclaim your time and your peace.

The High Cost of the Endless Scroll

Dating app burnout is a documented state of emotional and physical exhaustion. Recent surveys show that 78% of users report feeling "swiped out." For Gen Z, that number reaches 79%. For Millennials, it hits 80%. Women experience this fatigue more sharply than men.

The numbers explain the drain. The average user spends 51 minutes every day on these platforms. Millennials spend even more, averaging 56 minutes. That is nearly an hour a day swiping through strangers and managing dry conversations. Over a year, you spend 300 hours on a task that often yields no reward.

This labor is not accidental. The dating app industry is worth over $6 billion. These companies do not profit when you find love and delete their app. They profit when you stay. They monetize your loneliness. They optimize their systems for engagement, not for outcomes. They want you searching and subscribed, even if it leaves you exhausted.

The Rejection Mindset

As you view more profiles, your brain changes how it processes people. Researchers call this the "rejection mindset." A 2020 study found that your chance of accepting a match drops as you continue to swipe. On average, the likelihood of saying "yes" declines by 27% from the first profile to the last.

Why does this happen? Your brain becomes overwhelmed by the sheer volume of choices. To cope with the data, you start looking for reasons to say "no." You focus on small flaws instead of positive traits. You become a harsh judge rather than a curious seeker. This pessimism makes the whole process feel futile. It kills the excitement of meeting someone new.

This environment trains you to treat intimacy as a transaction. When options seem infinite, commitment feels like a risk. You worry that something "better" is only one swipe away. This is the "paradox of choice." Too many options lead to less satisfaction. You stop valuing the person in front of you because you think the pool is bottomless.

The Impact on Your Mental Health

Dating app fatigue is a major hurdle for your well-being. Studies from 2025 show that 58% of daters believe these apps negatively impact their mental health. Frequent rejection and ambiguous experiences like ghosting increase anxiety and self-doubt.

The constant focus on appearance erodes self-esteem. Women often report high levels of body image dissatisfaction after long periods of swiping. You start to tie your worth to your match count. If you don't get a notification, you feel invisible.

This cycle can lead to "learned helplessness." After repeated disappointments, you start to believe that nothing works. You feel that you will never find a connection. This is a survival signal from your nervous system. Your body is telling you that the digital environment is no longer safe or productive.

The "Readiness Gap" and High Standards

There is a growing gap between what we want and how we feel. Data from the 2025 Human Connection Study reveals a "readiness gap" among young singles. About 80% of Gen Z daters believe they will find true love. However, only 55% feel prepared for a real relationship.

This hesitation stems from pressure. You feel you must be a "final product" before you date. You want to have your finances, your therapy, and your boundaries perfect first. While self-growth is good, it can lead to paralysis. You wait for a level of readiness that never quite arrives.

The apps amplify this. They teach you to avoid the "messiness" of human interaction. You want a perfect match without the friction of a real date. Intimacy requires vulnerability and discomfort. The goal of dating is not to find a flaw-free person. The goal is to find a responsive partner.

Strategies to Reclaim Your Energy

You do not have to be a victim of the algorithm. You can change how you use these tools to protect your peace. Use these evidence-based steps to beat the burnout.

1. **Implement Strict Time Management:** Treat the app like a utility, not a hobby. Dedicate 15 or 20 minutes in the evening to respond to messages. Stop "boredom swiping" throughout the day. This prevents the dopamine loops from taking over your brain.
2. **Limit Your Conversations:** Focus on quality over quantity. Limit yourself to three active chats at a time. This allows for real curiosity and deeper engagement. It makes the process feel human rather than transactional.
3. **Get Offline Fast:** Use the app to get to the human quickly. Ask for a voice note or a quick video call within the first week. This restores social cues that text messages lack. If the interest is real, meet in person.
4. **Schedule "Analog Days":** Take regular breaks. Delete the apps for a weekend or a full week every month. Reconnect with your community and your hobbies. This allows your reward system to reset and reduces your dependence on digital validation.
5. **Change the Date Format:** Stop the "job interview" dates. Go for a walk in a park or visit a bookstore. Add an element of play to your meetings. Even if the date does not lead to a relationship, the experience should still add value to your day.

Choosing Slowness in a Fast Culture

In our current world, speed is often confused with progress. Real bonds take time to grow. Choosing slowness is a sign of self-respect. It allows you to observe behavior and consistency over time.

A priority partner will not mind a slower pace. He will respect your boundaries around your time and energy. He will show up with clarity instead of ambiguity. If someone disappears because you won't rush, let them. They are looking for convenience, not a connection.

You are the driver of your dating life. You decide when to open the app and when to close it. You decide who gets your energy. The moment you stop swiping for validation, you start swiping for value. You are the prize. Start acting like it today.

REFLECTION EXERCISES

CHAPTERS 1 TO 4

These exercises help you move from theory into action. You will apply the science and tools from the first four chapters to your own life. These drills use techniques from Cognitive Behavioral Therapy (CBT) and Dialectical Behavior Therapy (DBT). They help you rewire your brain and break the "option" cycle. Write your answers by hand in a journal. Research shows that hand-writing engages your motor cortex and helps you process hard emotions better than typing.

Chapter 1: Start Choosing Yourself

Chapter 1 looked at the "slot machine" effect and the math of your relationship value. These exercises help you see the raw truth of your current bond. They give you the tools to stop playing a game you cannot win.

Exercise 1.1: The Relational Value Ledger

Social Exchange Theory uses a simple formula to track the health of a bond: $Value = Rewards - Costs$. When you act as an option, the costs are almost always higher than the rewards. Use this table to find your current balance.

1. **Concrete Rewards:** List every positive thing he has done for you in the last 30 days. Include only actions, not promises or "potential." Did he take you on a planned date? Did he offer real help when you were sick? Do not include "he was nice on the phone once."
2. **Concrete Costs:** List the energy you spent on him. How many hours did you wait for a reply? How many times did you feel anxious or sick because of his silence? How many plans did you cancel to be ready for his last-minute text?
3. **The Verdict:** Subtract the costs from the rewards. If your number is zero or less, you are paying for a connection that drains you. Write down how it feels to see this math on paper. Why do you continue to pay this price?

Exercise 1.2: The Withdrawal Diary

Intermittent reinforcement makes your brain crave his attention like a drug. You are not in love; you are in withdrawal.

1. **The Trigger:** Describe the last time he reached out after days of silence. What was the exact message?
2. **The Physiological High:** What happened in your body the moment you saw his name? Did your heart race? Did your hands shake? This is a dopamine spike. It is a survival signal, not a sign of a soulmate.
3. **The Crash:** How long did that relief last? When did the doubt return? Note the time between the text and your next feeling of anxiety.
4. **The Reframing:** Read this out loud: "My brain is seeking relief from a withdrawal. This feeling is a chemical loop, not a romantic bond." How does this change your view of your "chemistry" with him?

Exercise 1.3: The "Let Them" Inventory

The "Let Them" Theory by Mel Robbins helps you stop trying to fix or manage him. You reclaim your energy by letting people be exactly who they choose to be.

1. **The Management List:** What behaviors of his are you trying to control? Are you trying to "make" him text more? Are you trying to "teach" him how to be a partner?
2. **The Detachment Practice:** Pick one behavior from your list. Write down what would happen if you said, "Let him." If he wants to ignore my text for three days, let him. If he wants to prioritize his friends every single night, let him.
3. **The Pivot:** Where can you put that saved energy right now? List three things you love doing that have nothing to do with a man. How does it feel to let go of the role of his teacher or manager?

Exercise 1.4: The Self-Priority Pledge

You stop being an option when you realize you are the prize. Use the FAST skill from DBT to evaluate your recent talks with him.

- **Fair:** Were you fair to your own needs in your last talk? Or did you minimize your feelings to keep the peace?
- **Apologies:** Did you apologize for asking for clarity? Did you say "sorry" for having a standard?
- **Stick to Values:** What is one value you compromised to stay in this connection? (e.g., honesty, consistency, or respect).
- **Truthful:** Did you make up excuses for his behavior? Write down the raw truth of his actions instead.
- **Action:** Write a pledge to yourself. "I will not accept because I value my peace more than his presence."

Chapter 2: Recognize Digital Mind Games

Your inbox is the front line for your heart. This section helps you identify the tactics he uses to keep you on standby. You will learn to trust your body's reaction to his silence.

Exercise 2.1: The Digital Detective Audit

Look at your last five digital interactions with him. Use the definitions from Chapter 2 to label his behavior.

1. **Is it a "Crumb"?:** Was it a low-effort signal like an emoji or a "like" without a real question?
2. **Is it "Banksying"?:** Did he send a vague link or a sad song lyric at 2:00 a.m. hoping you would "get it"?
3. **Is it "Ghostlighting"?:** Did he vanish for a week and then return while acting like you are "too intense" for noticing the gap?
4. **The Effort Score:** On a scale of 1-10, how much effort did he put into these messages? On a scale of 1-10, how much energy did you spend trying to decode them? If your score is higher, you are doing the emotional heavy lifting.

Exercise 2.2: Somatic Data Collection

Your brain processes digital silence like a physical burn. Rejection lights up the dorsal anterior cingulate cortex (dACC).

1. **The Situation:** Think about a time you saw a "seen" receipt but received no reply for hours.
2. **Locate the Sensation:** Where do you feel the sting? Is it a knot in your stomach? A tightness in your chest? A headache?
3. **The Message:** What is this pain trying to tell you about your safety in this connection?
4. **The Regulatory Response:** Take five deep, slow breaths. As you exhale, say: "This pain is a signal that my environment is inconsistent. I am safe now, and I can choose how to respond."

Exercise 2.3: The Notification Detox Protocol

You can break the addiction to your phone through structure. Use these steps to reset your reward system.

1. **The Silent Rule:** Turn off notifications for his thread. commit to checking it only twice a day (e.g., 8:00 a.m. and 8:00 p.m.).

2. **The 60-Minute Timer:** If he sends a vague text, set a timer for 60 minutes before you look at it. What did you do with that hour? How did it feel to be the one who controls the clock?
3. **The App Purge:** Delete your dating apps for 48 hours. Write down what you felt during those two days. Were you anxious? Relieved? Bored?
4. **The Log:** Keep a record of your phone-checking urges for three days. What emotions precede the urge to check on him?

Exercise 2.4: The Assertive Clarity Script

Practice demanding a "yes" or "no" answer using the DEAR MAN technique. This removes digital ambiguity.

1. **Describe:** State the facts. "We have been talking for two weeks, but we haven't met."
2. **Express:** Share the feeling. "I feel disconnected when we only text."
3. **Assert:** Be direct. "I would like to go on a date this Friday at 7:00 p.m. Are you free?"
4. **Reinforce:** Explain the gain. "This will help me see if we have real chemistry."
5. **The Result:** If he gives a vague answer, he is not a priority partner. Write down how it feels to have that data immediately instead of waiting for a "maybe" all week.

Chapter 3: End the Search for Sparse Validation

This section focuses on your "sociometer" and the "mattering deficit." You will practice self-validation and move away from performing for others to get a "high."

Exercise 3.1: The Mattering Audit (N.A.N. Framework)

Zach Mercurio defines mattering through three signs: being Noticed, Affirmed, and Needed.

1. **The External Audit:** In your current connection, does he notice your needs without you having to beg? Does he affirm your unique traits? Does he treat you as someone needed for his life to be whole?

2. **The Internal Audit:** How can you provide these for yourself today?
   - **Notice:** List one physical need you have right now (e.g., rest, a walk, water). Meet it.
   - **Affirm:** List three things you did well today that no one saw.
   - **Need:** Remind yourself why you are essential to your own goals. Write: "I need myself to be healthy so I can achieve."
3. **The Shift:** How would your life change if you stopped waiting for him to provide these three things?

Exercise 3.2: Reassurance Compulsion vs. Self-Security

If you ask "Are we okay?" multiple times a day, you may have a reassurance compulsion.

1. **Identify the Urge:** When you feel the need to ask for validation or reassurance, stop.
2. **Delay the Ask:** Set a timer for 30 minutes. Sit with the anxiety. Use slow, deep breaths to calm your heart rate.
3. **Accept Uncertainty:** Say out loud: "I cannot be 100% sure how he feels right now, and that is okay. My worth is not tied to his mood."
4. **The Outcome:** Did the anxiety fade after the timer? Most urges pass if you wait 30 minutes. Record how many times you successfully delayed the urge today.

Exercise 3.3: Truecasting vs. The Mask

We often hide our real needs to avoid appearing "too much." This is a facade that leads to unfulfilling situationships.

1. **The Mask List:** What parts of your personality do you hide from him? Do you hide your desire for a family? Do you hide your need for daily check-ins?
2. **The Fear:** What are you afraid will happen if you show the real you? Be specific.
3. **The Priority Shift:** A priority partner wants the real you. Write down one "Truth" about your needs that you will share in your next talk. If he leaves, he was never your person.

4. **The Reflection:** How does it feel to be "liked" for a version of yourself that isn't real? Is that reward worth the cost of your authenticity?

Exercise 3.4: The Mirror Talk Drill

Looking into your own eyes with kindness is a direct reaffirmation of self-worth.

1. **The Action:** Stand in front of a mirror. Look into your eyes for two minutes without looking away.
2. **The Affirmation:** Say five things out loud that you love about your personality. Use "I" statements (e.g., "I love that I am a loyal friend"). Do not mention your looks.
3. **The Commitment:** Say, "I see you. You matter. I am choosing you today."
4. **The Reflection:** How did this feel? If it felt awkward or painful, your "internal validation" muscles are weak. Practice this every morning for seven days. Record any changes in your mood or self-perception.

Chapter 4: Face the Reality of Online Dating Fatigue

This section addresses the "rejection mindset" and the "readiness gap." You will create a structure for your digital life that protects your mental health.

Exercise 4.1: The Rejection Mindset Check

Studies show that swiping through many profiles makes you focus on flaws instead of traits. You become a harsh judge to cope with the volume of data.

1. **The 27% Rule:** Remind yourself that your chance of matching drops by 27% as you continue to swipe. Your brain is training itself to say "no."
2. **The Focus Shift:** Open your app. Look at the next three profiles. Instead of looking for a reason to reject them, find one interesting trait in each person.
3. **The Limit:** Close the app after looking at only ten profiles. How does your brain feel compared to a one-hour swiping session?

4. **The Diagnostic:** On a scale of 1-10, how cynical do you feel about men after swiping? If your score is above a 5, it is time for a break.

Exercise 4.2: The Readiness Gap Audit

Many women feel they must be "perfect" before they are ready for a relationship. This leads to paralysis.

1. **The "Prerequisite" List:** Write down the things you think you need to have perfect before you date (e.g., "lose 10 pounds," "get a promotion," "finish my therapy").
2. **The Reality Check:** Which of these are truly necessary for a healthy bond? Which are just ways to avoid the "messiness" of human connection?
3. **The Action Step:** Intimacy requires responsiveness, not perfection. Write down one way you can show up as a "work in progress" on your next date.
4. **The Value Shift:** List three qualities you bring to a relationship *right now* that have nothing to do with your career or your appearance.

Exercise 4.3: The App Time-Box

Treat your dating apps like a utility, not a hobby or a source of validation.

1. **Set the Schedule:** Pick two 15-minute windows in your day to handle messages. Outside of these times, the apps are off-limits.
2. **The Quality Cap:** Limit yourself to three active conversations at a time. This prevents "cognitive overload" and decision fatigue.
3. **The Analog Goal:** What will you do with the 45 minutes you saved today? Make a plan for that time now. (e.g., call a friend, read a book, take a walk).
4. **The Notification Check:** Are your notifications still on? Turn them off now. Check the apps on your terms, not the algorithm's terms.

Exercise 4.4: Redefining Date Success

Stop using dates as "job interviews." This contributes to burnout and fatigue.

1. **The Play Plan:** Instead of coffee or drinks, suggest a date that involves movement or an activity (e.g., a walk in a park, a bookstore visit, or a trivia night).
2. **The Goal Change:** Shift your goal from "finding the one" to "having a new experience."
3. **The Post-Date Reflection:** After the date, do not ask "Did he like me?". Ask these four questions:
   - Did this interaction feel respectful?
   - Did I feel seen and heard?
   - Did this conversation energize me or drain me?
   - Was I able to be my real self?
4. **The Verdict:** If the answer to any of these is "no," there is no need for a second date. Respect your own data.

Your future starts with your notebook. By answering these questions, you are training your brain to prioritize your own peace over his validation. You are moving from a reactive state to a proactive one. You are choosing yourself. Keep going. The clarity you seek is already within you.

PART TWO

THE HIDDEN MAP OF THE PAST

CHAPTER 5

LINK YOUR PAST WOUNDS TO YOUR PRESENT CHOICES

You meet a man and the attraction hits you like a lightning strike. You call it chemistry. You tell your friends that you have finally found a "spark." This feeling is intense and magnetic. You feel like you have known him forever. Science suggests a darker truth about that instant bond. Often, that "spark" is not a sign of a soulmate. It is the sound of an old wound recognizing a familiar source of pain.

Your brain uses an internal map to find love. This map was drawn before you could even read. It was created through your early bonds with your parents or caregivers. If those bonds were shaky or cold, your map is flawed. It leads you toward people who mirror that early neglect.

You do not choose him because he is good for you. You choose him because he feels like "home." This chapter looks at how your past dictates your present. We examine the facts on attachment styles and core wounds. You will learn to spot the familiarity trap that keeps you stuck as an option. You will learn how to redraw your map so it leads to a partner who chooses you first.

The Invisible Blueprint of Age Five

Your internal model of relationships forms before you reach age five. During these early years, your brain is a sponge for social data. You learn what to expect from other people. You learn how much your needs matter. If your parents were consistent and warm, you develop a secure attachment style. You grow up expecting respect and reliability. You do not tolerate people who ignore you because you know you are valuable.

Many children do not receive this consistency. About 40% of adults possess an insecure attachment style. This happens when caregivers are emotionally absent or unpredictable. A child's brain is wired for survival. If care is sporadic, the child learns to "hunt" for it. They become hyper-vigilant. They scan for moods and shifts in tone. They learn that love is something you must earn through performance or silence.

Why does his distance make you work harder? It is because your brain recognizes the silence as a familiar childhood pattern. You are trying to "fix" the original wound by winning over this new, unavailable person. You believe that if you can make him choose you, you will finally prove that you are worthy of love. This is a biological cycle, not a romantic one. Your brain is replaying a script that was written decades ago.

The Familiarity Trap and the Brain

People are not always drawn to what is safe. They are drawn to what is emotionally familiar. A 2015 review in *Frontiers in Psychology* explains this paradox. Early experiences shape what your nervous system perceives as "normal." If you grew up in a home with low emotional availability, steady love may feel strange. It might even feel boring. You may shun healthy partners because they lack the "anxiety spark" you have been trained to expect.

You confuse the stomach knots of uncertainty with the butterflies of love. When a partner pulls away, your brain enters a state of alarm. You cling harder. You double your efforts to communicate. You accept "crumbs" because they feel like a victory in a familiar war. This is your subconscious attachment template running the show. It fires in milliseconds. You are not making a logical choice. You are reacting to a map that is leading you back into the forest.

A 2025 study on relational value shows that the brain tracks how much others value us through two paths. One path looks at rewards, like a nice text. The second path builds an internal model of our worth. In an "option" dynamic, these paths split. You get rare rewards that do not match your low relational value. This creates a "reward prediction error" that keeps you hooked. Your brain becomes obsessed with closing the gap between the crumbs you get and the love you want.

The Four Blueprints of Attachment

To break the cycle, you must know which map you are using. Psychologists identify four main attachment styles. Each one has a specific "core wound" that drives your choices in dating.

1. **Secure Attachment:** You feel comfortable with intimacy. You do not worry about being alone. You choose partners who are consistent and kind.
2. **Anxious-Preoccupied:** Your core wound is a fear of abandonment. You equate uncertainty with passion. When he pulls away, you go into "protest behavior." You text more. You check his social media. You try to "fix" the distance because the silence feels like death.
3. **Dismissive-Avoidant:** Your core wound is a fear of losing your autonomy. You act like a "self-sufficient fortress." You take pride in not needing anyone. You use distance as a shield. You leave before things get "too serious" to avoid being rejected first.
4. **Fearful-Avoidant:** Your core wound is a fear of betrayal. You want closeness, but you do not trust it. You cycle between being very intense and suddenly withdrawing. You are often drawn to chaotic and toxic dynamics because they match your internal state.

If you have an anxious style, you are often drawn to the avoidant fortress. You want to be the person who finally makes him open up. You think your love will be the key that unlocks his heart. His walls are not about you. They are about his internal model of safety. You cannot love someone into being available if their brain views closeness as a threat to their survival.

The Biology of Emotional Neglect

Childhood Emotional Neglect (CEN) leaves a physical mark on the body. About 1 in 5 adults globally may have been neglected as a child. This often happens unintentionally when parents are busy or depressed. The absence of emotional engagement leaves children feeling invisible and unimportant. This injures your sense of self and makes you distrustful of others.

The impact is chemical. Infants with emotionally unavailable mothers show higher baseline levels of cortisol. Cortisol is the body's primary stress hormone. However, these same infants show a *lower* cortisol response to actual separation. This indicates a state of physiological shutdown. They have learned that crying does not bring help, so they stop reacting.

This suppression follows you into adulthood. You might feel "numb" or "dead" when you are mistreated. You might not even realize you are being treated like an option. Your body learned to survive neglect long ago. You have a "high distress tolerance" for the wrong things. You tolerate silence and inconsistency because your nervous system thinks this is the only way to stay safe.

The Identity Crisis and the Default Mode Network

Trauma can fragment your sense of self. When you spend your life trying to get an unavailable person to notice you, you lose your own identity. You become a "service zone" for their needs. Recent research from 2025 and 2026 highlights the role of the Default Mode Network (DMN) in the brain. This network handles self-reflection and memory.

In people with a history of relational trauma, the DMN becomes intimately linked to the memories of rejection. You stop knowing who you are outside of your "struggle" to be loved. You feel "invisible" or "like an object" rather than a person. You may find yourself constantly on alert, even when nothing is wrong. This hyper-vigilance is not a personality trait. it is a protective response your brain practiced to survive your past.

Why do we feel so lost after a breakup with an unavailable man? It is because we have tied our entire identity to the quest for his validation. When he leaves, the quest ends, and we are left with a void. To heal, you must decouple your sense of self from the "option" dynamic. You must move from being a responder to his crumbs to being the creator of your own life.

Redrawing Your Internal Map

Redrawing your map starts with radical acceptance. You must acknowledge the reality of your childhood without blame. Healing is your responsibility. You have the power of neuroplasticity. This is your brain's ability to form new neural pathways and unlearn old habits. You can teach your brain that consistency is safe and anxiety is a warning sign.

The "Who Am I Becoming?" Practice

Journaling is a tool to reclaim your voice. When trauma shapes your identity, you lose sight of your own desires. Use this practice to engage your prefrontal cortex. Ask yourself two questions today. What parts of me did I hide to survive my past? Who am I choosing to become now that I am safe enough to grow? Write your answers by hand. This engages your motor cortex and helps you process the information more deeply.

The Inner Child Comfort Ritual

Find a quiet space and close your eyes. Imagine yourself as a small child who felt unseen or ignored. Visualize your current, adult self kneeling down to embrace that child. Tell her, "Your feelings are valid. You are important. I am here to listen to you now." This exercise signals safety to your nervous system. it helps you "re-parent" yourself. You stop looking for a partner to fill the void of your past. You start providing that validation for yourself. This reduces your hunger for his crumbs.

Identifying the "Option" Template in Dating

Look at your dating history with raw honesty. Do you see a pattern? You might notice that you consistently choose people who are "half-in." You choose the man who is still grieving an ex. You choose the man who is "too busy" for a commitment. These are not accidents. They are attempts to recreate a childhood dynamic where love was earned, not given.

Stop asking, "Why won't he choose me?". Start asking, "Why am I choosing a person who is not choosing me?". This shift in perspective gives you back your agency. You move from being a victim of his behavior to being the director of your own life. You show people how to treat you by what you accept. If you accept being an option, you are reinforcing your old, flawed map. You are telling your brain that the old pain is still your only choice.

You must learn to value peace over the rush of the chase. A healthy relationship is not a puzzle to be solved. it is a partnership that feels solid and reliable. If a person does not offer consistency, they are not a match for your new map. Let them go. You are clearing space for someone who wants to give you the whole meal.

Exercises to Break the Familiarity Trap

You can rewire your attraction through consistent cognitive drills. These tools help you move out of your "emotional brain" and into your "logical brain."

1. **The "Anxiety vs. Chemistry" Audit:** Next time you feel a "spark," pause. Rate your anxiety on a scale of 1-10. Is the feeling one of peace or one of uncertainty? If your anxiety is high, the "spark" is likely a trauma response.
2. **Identify Your Non-Negotiables:** Write a list of what you require in a relationship. Consistency, honesty, and respect should be at the top. If a person cannot meet these in the first month, they do not get a second month.
3. **Practice Emotional Awareness:** Set a timer for three times a day. Ask yourself, "What am I feeling right now?". Name the emotion out loud. This engages your prefrontal cortex and helps you regulate your responses.

4. **Mirror Work for Self-Worth:** Stand in front of a mirror and look into your own eyes. Say, "I see you. You matter. I am choosing you today." This builds internal validation and reduces your need for external applause.

Living as a New Priority

Your past is a chapter in your book, but it is not the whole story. You now see that your attraction to unavailable men is a biological echo. It is a sign that your inner child is still hunting for approval. You have the tools to heal that wound. You can name your emotions. You can set boundaries. You can build a sense of self that does not rely on his "likes" or texts.

When you heal your early wounds, your "type" will change. You will find that inconsistent people no longer interest you. You will be drawn to those who are clear and reliable. You stop being an option the moment you decide that your "home" will be built on respect, not neglect.

Stop waiting for a text that only gives you crumbs. Start living a life that offers you everything you deserve. The path away from the forest is open. You have the map, and you have the strength to walk it. Choose yourself today and every day after.

CHAPTER 6

SPOT THE PARTNER WHO BUILDS HIGH WALLS

You sit across from a man who seems to have everything together. He has a steady job and a sharp wit. He tells you that he is a "lone wolf." He says he values his freedom and does not like "drama." At first, this feels like strength. It feels like he is a man who knows himself. Weeks later, you realize you are screaming into a void. You are trying to climb a wall that has no top. You are dating a partner who builds high walls.

This partner is often called a Dismissive Avoidant. He is physically present but emotionally absent. He treats intimacy like a cage. When you get too close, he disappears. This behavior is not a mystery. It is a biological pattern. This chapter looks at the science of the "fortress" partner. We examine the latest data from 2024 and 2025. You will learn to spot the signs before you waste months trying to "fix" a man who does not want to be found. You will find the tools to choose a partner who is ready to be seen.

The Neurobiology of the Wall

Dismissive avoidant attachment is not just a choice. It is a way the brain is wired. Research published in 2024 in *Nature Reviews Neuroscience* shows a clear difference in how these individuals process connection. Most people have a reward system that lights up during moments of comfort. When you see a photo of a loved one, your ventral striatum and amygdala activate. You feel a "high" from the bond.

Dismissive avoidants do not have this response. Brain imaging reveals that their reward circuits stay quiet when they view scenes of safety or connection. Their prefrontal cortex, the analytical part of the brain, works overtime instead. They are thinking and analyzing rather than feeling. Their nervous system treats your attempt at closeness as a threat. They do not feel a rush of love. They feel a rush of "engulfment."

This is why he pulls away after a great date. The "high" you felt was a "low" for him. His brain signaled that his autonomy was in danger. He uses "deactivating strategies" to turn off his attachment system. He focuses on your flaws. He tells himself he is better off alone. This is his way of regaining a sense of safety. He built these neural pathways in childhood to survive neglect, and now he uses them to survive you.

Identifying the " Lone Wolf" Prototype

To protect your heart, you must recognize the signs of a wall-builder early. These partners often follow a specific script. They present a version of themselves that is attractive and stable, but they lack the capacity for depth.

1. The History of Short-Term "Ships"

A history of short-term relationships is a major red flag. A person who is emotionally available has a record of building bonds. A wall-builder has a record of escape. He might tell you that his exes were all "crazy" or "too needy." In reality, he likely left the moment the relationship required real vulnerability. He prefers "situationships" or casual dating because they have no labels and no requirements.

2. Intellectualizing Emotions

When you talk about feelings, he talks about facts. He might analyze your emotions like a math problem. He uses logic to avoid the messiness of the heart. If you tell him you are hurt, he explains why you should not feel that way. This is a defense mechanism. By keeping the talk at a mental level, he never has to touch the emotional layer.

3. The Intimacy Hangover

This is a classic sign. You have a wonderful, vulnerable weekend together. You feel closer than ever. Then, he goes silent for four days. This is the "intimacy hangover." The closeness was too much for his nervous system. He needs to retreat into his "fortress" to feel like himself again. He is not busy. He is recovering from the "threat" of your connection.

4. Excessive Self-Reliance

He prides himself on not needing anyone. He does not ask for help. He does not share his struggles. He might even view your need for support as a weakness. This self-reliance is a mask for a deep fear of being let down. If he never depends on you, you can never hurt him. This also means he can never truly love you.

The Science of Stonewalling

One of the most damaging behaviors of a wall-builder is stonewalling. This happens when a partner shuts down during a talk and breaks eye contact. He stops responding. He might walk out of the room. This is not just a bad habit. It is a survival response.

Dr. John Gottman's research shows that 85% of stonewallers are men. During a conflict, their heart rate often spikes above 100 beats per minute. This is called "physiological flooding." Their body enters a state of fight-or-flight. Because they cannot fight you and they cannot leave the house, they "freeze." They shut down their emotions to survive the stress.

The problem is that stonewalling is a primary predictor of divorce. It blocks any chance of solving a problem. It leaves you feeling abandoned and alone. For the wall-builder, the silence is a shield. For you, the silence is a weapon. If a partner repeatedly uses the silent treatment to manage his stress, he is not emotionally ready for a relationship. He is managing his own internal storm at your expense.

The Anxious-Avoidant Trap

If you have an anxious attachment style, you are the natural target for a wall-builder. This is the "anxious-avoidant dance." You want closeness. He wants distance. The more you chase him to get validation, the faster he runs to get safety.

This dynamic creates a cycle of "intermittent reinforcement." He gives you a tiny crumb of attention. You feel a dopamine spike. Then he pulls away, and you enter a state of withdrawal. You spend all your time trying to "figure him out." You become a detective for his moods. This makes you feel like you are in an intense romance, but you are actually in a chemical loop.

Why do you stay? It is often because you believe you can be the one to change him. You think your love will be the key to his fortress. Science is clear: a person only changes their attachment style through long-term, intentional work. You cannot love a man into being available. His walls were built before he knew you. They are not your responsibility to tear down.

Screening Tests for the First Month

You do not have to wait six months to find out if a man is a wall-builder. You can use specific tests in the first few weeks to see his capacity for intimacy.

1. **The Vulnerability Test:** Share a small, real fear or a minor struggle. See how he reacts. Does he offer empathy? Or does he change the subject? A wall-builder will feel uncomfortable and try to "fix" it or ignore it.
2. **The Needs Test:** State a clear need. "I really value daily check-ins. It makes me feel connected." See if he can meet that need consistently. If he calls it "intense" or fails to follow through, he is telling you his limit.
3. **The "Why" Test:** Ask about his longest relationship and why it ended. If he takes no responsibility and blames the other person's "neediness," pay attention. This shows a lack of self-awareness.
4. **The Boundary Test:** Say "no" to a plan he suggests. A healthy partner will respect your choice. A wall-builder may feel relieved

that he has his night back, or he may use it as a reason to go silent for a week.

Breaking the Pattern of "Potential"

We often fall in love with a man's potential rather than his reality. You see the man he *could* be if he just let go of his fear. You see the "good version" of him that shows up once a month. You cannot date a man's potential. You must date the man who is standing in front of you today.

If he is standing behind a wall today, he will be behind a wall next year. In 2026, emotional maturity is the highest form of value in dating. A man who cannot state his intentions or manage his fears is not a "lone wolf." He is an emotionally stunted partner.

You deserve a partner who is an open book, not a secret code. You deserve someone who views your closeness as a reward, not a threat. Stop being a worker on his walls. Start being the architect of your own peace.

Practical Steps to Protect Your Peace

If you realize you are dating a wall-builder, you have three choices. You can accept the crumbs. You can try to fight the walls. Or you can walk away.

1. **Use the "Let Them" Framework:** If he wants to be distant, let him. If he wants to ignore your text, let him. Stop the chase. Watch what he does when you stop providing the energy for the connection. If he disappears, he was never there to begin with.
2. **Set a Time Limit:** Give yourself a deadline. If he does not show a real change in consistency within 30 days, leave. Do not give him "just one more chance."
3. **Practice Opposite Action:** When you feel the urge to text him after he pulls away, do the opposite. Call a friend. Go to the gym. Focus on your own life. This breaks the chemical hook and restores your agency.
4. **Identify the "Spark" for What It Is:** Remind yourself that the intense attraction you feel is likely "anxiety chemistry." It is the sound of your old wounds. Choose peace over passion.

Conclusion: Living Outside the Fortress

True intimacy requires two people who are willing to be seen. A wall-builder is a person who is hiding. You cannot build a home with someone who is constantly looking for the exit.

When you stop trying to climb his walls, you finally see the wide world around you. You realize that you are the prize. You do not need to prove your worth to a man who is too scared to see it.

The path to a priority relationship starts with choosing a partner who is already standing in the light. Put down your tools. Walk away from the fortress. Your life is waiting for you on the other side.

CHAPTER 7

CALM THE FEAR OF BEING ALONE

You stay because you fear the quiet. You stay because the thought of an empty Saturday night feels like a cold wind against your skin. You accept the crumbs of his attention because you think a tiny bit of love is better than none at all. When he stops texting, you feel a pit in your stomach. This is not just a mood. It is a primal alarm. Your brain treats the prospect of being alone as a threat to your very life.

This fear is often why you settle for being an option. It acts as the anchor that keeps you tied to a man who does not choose you. 2026 research shows that being alone and being lonely are not the same thing. In this chapter, we look at the evolutionary biology of your fear. We examine the latest data from 2025 on how culture trains you to hate solitude. You will learn to silence the survival alarm in your head. You will find the tools to build "positive solitude" so you can choose a partner from a place of want, not a place of desperation.

The Tribe and the Saber-Toothed Tiger

Your brain is an ancient organ living in a modern world. For our ancestors, being alone meant certain death. If you were kicked out of the tribe, you had no one to help you hunt or stay warm. You were an easy target for predators. Because of this, humans evolved a "social body" that needs connection just as much as the physical body needs water.

Evolutionary psychologist John Cacioppo spent years studying this signal. He argued that loneliness is a biological hunger. It is an aversive signal designed to make you reconnect with others for your own survival. When you feel the pang of being alone, your brain is actually trying to protect you. It is saying, "Go back to the group or you will die."

In 2026, this alarm still goes off. It goes off when you see your friends post photos of a dinner you were not invited to. It goes off when you face a weekend without a date. There are no saber-toothed tigers in your living room. The alarm is outdated. To stop being an option, you must recognize that your physical safety no longer depends on a man's validation. You can pay your own bills and buy your own groceries. You are safe, even if you are solo.

The Brain's Fire Alarm: The Anterior Cingulate Cortex

Why does the fear of being alone feel like physical pain?. It is because your brain uses the same hardware for both. Scans show that social exclusion activates the dorsal anterior cingulate cortex (dACC). This is the region that processes the "distressing" part of an injury. When he leaves you on "read," your brain feels a sting similar to a burn or a cut.

This "social pain network" is why you might feel sick when you think about a breakup. You might experience a leaden feeling in your chest or a knot in your gut. This is your nervous system entering a state of hyper-vigilance. You start scanning for social threats. You become more sensitive to rejection.

A 2025 study in the *Journal of Affective Disorders* found that people with high "sensory processing sensitivity" feel this even more sharply. Their brains work harder to process every interaction. They need more time alone to recover, yet their survival alarm tells them that being alone is dangerous. This creates a cycle of stress. To break it, you must learn to regulate your dACC through mindfulness and slow, deep breathing.

The Loneliness Paradox and the Media

We live in a culture that hates being alone. A University of Michigan study from February 2025 looked at 144 news articles from leading U.S. papers. They found that solitude is depicted as a negative state ten times more often than as a benefit. The media warns us that being alone leads to disease, depression, and early death.

This creates a "loneliness paradox." If you believe that being alone is harmful, you will feel lonelier when you are by yourself. Your mindset dictates your experience. If you view an empty house as a sign of failure, your body will release cortisol. If you view it as a sanctuary for growth, your body stays calm.

In 2026, we are seeing a shift. Many women are reclaiming solitude. They are realizing that being unpartnered allows for "individuation." This is the process of becoming your true self without having to compromise for someone else. When you stop viewing singlehood as a "temporary problem" to be fixed, the fear starts to fade. You move from being an involuntary single to a voluntary one.

Positive Solitude vs. Chronic Loneliness

Solitude and loneliness are two different things. Solitude is a choice. It is a state of being alone that is invigorating and restorative. Loneliness is a perception of being unimportant or unwanted. It is a state of being alone that is painful and agonizing.

Feature	Solitude (Strength)	Loneliness (Pain)
Choice	Voluntary and desired	Involuntary and feared
Mindset	Opportunity for growth	Sign of personal failure
Effect	Enhances creativity and self-awareness	Increases stress and inflammation
Outcome	Leads to better relationships	Leads to dependency and settling

A 2026 study in the *Journal of Personality and Social Psychology* found that women who value their autonomy report higher life satisfaction when single than when in poor-quality relationships. They use their "One Time", time spent alone, to pursue passions that they once put aside. They build a solid internal foundation. This means they no longer need a man to tell them they are okay. They already know they are.

The Village of Support: Rebalancing Your Social Body

One reason the fear of being alone is so strong is that we expect one person to meet all our needs. We want a partner to be a lover, a best friend, a therapist, and a co-pilot. This is a very recent and unrealistic expectation. When that one person is inconsistent, our whole social world collapses.

To calm the fear, you must build a village. Data from 2025 shows that single women are generally happier than single men because they maintain stronger friendship networks. Women reach outward for connection, while men often turn inward.

Fostering platonic love reduces the pressure on your dating life. When you have friends who show up consistently, your oxytocin levels stay stable. Your survival brain feels safe. You realize that even if he does not text back, you still have a tribe. You are not "alone" in the evolutionary sense. This allows you to set firmer boundaries with unavailable men. You can afford to lose him because you have a world that is already full.

Unlearning the Fear: A Practical Guide

You can train your brain to feel at ease with itself. This requires gradual exposure and cognitive reframing. Use the following steps to build your "solitude muscles."

1. Identify the Root Cause

Ask yourself where the fear comes from. Was it a childhood where you felt ignored? Was it a past relationship where you were blindsided by a breakup?. Journaling about these memories helps you see that the fear is a ghost from the past, not a reality of the present.

2. Practice "Micro-Solitude"

If a whole weekend alone scares you, start small. Take yourself for a coffee for 15 minutes. Sit without your phone. Notice the sights and sounds around you. Next week, take a solo nature walk for 30 minutes. Gradually increase the time as your confidence grows.

3. Reframe the Silence

When the room is quiet, your brain might start telling you "I'm a loser" or "No one loves me." Challenge these thoughts. Replace them with fact-based statements: "I am having a quiet evening so I can rest. This is a choice for my own well-being."

4. Build a Comfort List

Create a list of activities that you can *only* do well alone. This might be reading a specific genre of book, painting, or watching a movie your ex hated. When you look forward to these activities, the fear of the empty weekend turns into anticipation.

5. Strengthen Your "Internal Sociometer"

Your worth is not a vote. It is a fact. Practice self-affirmation. Stand in front of a mirror and say, "I am a person of value. I am choosing my own company today." This signals to your nervous system that you are a safe person to be with.

The Solo Paradox

We often think we need a relationship to feel complete, but the paradox is that you are only ready for a healthy relationship when you don't *need* one to survive. If you are terrified of being alone, you will tolerate mistreatment. You will ignore red flags. You will stay an option because you are scared of the exit.

When you calm the fear, you gain a "superpower." You gain the ability to walk away. You can look a man in the eye and say, "I like you, but I don't like how you treat my time. I'd rather be alone than be an option." This clarity is magnetic to priority partners. It shows that you have high self-worth and healthy boundaries.

Conclusion: Reclaiming Your Sanctuary

Being alone is not a sentence. It is a sanctuary for self-discovery. You are the only person who will be with you for your entire life. It is time to make that relationship a priority.

The survival alarm in your head is just a biological echo. It is a memory of a time when the tribe was everything. In 2026, you are the tribe. You have the power to feed your own soul and protect your own peace. When you are no longer afraid of the quiet, you will never have to chase the crumbs of a "maybe" again. You will wait for the man who offers the whole meal, or you will happily eat alone. Either way, you win.

Scientific Note on the "Sociometer"

Mark Leary's sociometer theory suggests that self-esteem is an internal gauge of our relational value. When we are treated as an option, our sociometer drops, triggering anxiety. Rebuilding self-esteem requires moving the "source" of the gauge from others' opinions to our own values.

By focusing on internal metrics, you stabilize your mood and become more resilient to social rejection.

CHAPTER 8

COMFORT THE PART OF YOU THAT FEELS UNSEEN

You sit in a crowded room with him, but you feel like a ghost. He talks to everyone else. He laughs at their jokes. He looks past you as if you are part of the furniture. You wait for a look or a touch that says you are there. It never comes. This feeling of being invisible is a deep and heavy pain. It makes you feel small. It makes you feel like you do not matter. This is not just a bad date or a cold streak. It is a sign that you are living in the "service zone" of his life. You are a tool for his comfort, not a partner for his heart.

This chapter looks at the facts of being unseen. We examine the science of why you feel invisible and how to fix it. We use the latest data from 2025 and 2026 on "mattering" and brain health. You will find the tools to comfort the part of you that was ignored in the past. You will learn to move from seeking his gaze to valuing your own presence. You stop being a ghost the moment you decide to be seen by yourself.

The Search for Significance

Every person has a primal hunger to be significant to others. This is the core force that drives human behavior. Leadership researcher Zach Mercurio argue in his 2025 work that "mattering" is a biological requirement for health. He defines mattering through three specific signs: being Noticed, Affirmed, and Needed. This is the N.A.N. framework.

When you are an option, you lack these three things. He might notice you only when he needs a favor or a "hookup." He does not affirm your unique gifts. He does not treat you as someone essential to his world. This creates a "mattering deficit." You feel a sense of inadequacy and alienation.

Why do you stay with a man who does not see you? It is because you are trying to fill a void that started long ago. If you felt unseen as a child, you are trained to hunt for validation from people who withhold it. You believe that if you can finally make *him* see you, the old pain will vanish. This is a trap. You cannot get enough of what you do not actually need. You do not need his validation. You need your own.

The Neurobiology of the Invisible Child

Being unseen leaves a physical mark on the brain. When a child's emotional needs are ignored, the brain adapts to survive the silence. This is called Childhood Emotional Neglect (CEN). About 1 in 5 adults may have experienced this neglect. It often happens when parents are busy, depressed, or emotionally immature.

The impact is chemical. Infants with emotionally unavailable mothers show higher baseline levels of cortisol. This is the body's primary stress hormone. However, these same infants show a *lower* cortisol response to actual separation. This indicates a state of physiological shutdown. They have learned that expressing needs does not bring help, so they stop reacting.

In adulthood, this shows up as "emotional detachment." You might feel "numb" or "dead inside" when he ignores you. You have a high tolerance for neglect because your nervous system thinks this is the only way to stay safe. You repeat the role of the "invisible one" because it feels familiar. Your brain uses a map from the past that leads you toward people who mirror your original neglect.

The Default Mode Network and Identity

Trauma fragments your sense of self. fMRI scans from 2025 and 2026 highlight the role of the Default Mode Network (DMN) in this process. The DMN handles self-reflection and memory. In healthy people, it provides a stable sense of who they are across time.

In people with a history of neglect, the DMN becomes linked to memories of rejection. You stop knowing who you are outside of your "struggle" to be loved. You feel "like an object, not like a person." You spend so much energy managing his moods that you lose track of your own desires. You become a responder to his crumbs rather than the creator of your own life.

Breaking this cycle requires you to decouple your identity from the relationship. You must engage your prefrontal cortex to regulate your emotions. You must learn to name your feelings to bring your brain back "online." When you say, "I feel invisible right now," you stop being the feeling and start observing it. This is the first step toward reclaiming your voice.

Internal vs. External Validation: The Sugar Rush

Validation-seeking is the habit of needing others to affirm your worth. It is a survival mechanism. As kids, we needed belonging to stay safe. In adulthood, relying on external feedback is like living on a roller coaster that someone else is driving.

External validation is like a sugar rush. It gives you a quick spike of joy when he texts or likes a photo. The feeling is not lasting. When the silence returns, you crash back into doubt. You start asking, "Was I good enough?" or "Does he still like me?". This constant chasing of dopamine rewires your brain to rely on external triggers, which leaves you weaker at self-validation.

Internal validation is nourishment. It builds long-term strength. It comes from your own values and actions. Instead of asking, "Did he like my outfit?", you ask, "Did I feel confident in what I wore?". You move from being a consumer of his attention to being the architect of your own value.

Validation Type	Source	Result
External	His texts, moods, and "likes"	Anxiety and instability
Internal	Your values and personal goals	Peace and resilience

A study published in 2025 in the *Journal of Affective Disorders* found that how the brain learns from rewards predicts mental health. If you rely on external "hits" of praise, your nervous system stays in a state of alarm. To heal, you must strengthen your internal anchors.

The Reparenting Process

Healing from neglect starts with acknowledging your "wounded inner child." This is the part of you that needed love and attention but received only silence. Reconnecting with this part of yourself can feel strange at first, but it is essential for recovery.

The Inner Child Visualization

Find a quiet space and close your eyes. Imagine yourself as a small child who felt unseen. Visualize your adult self kneeling down to embrace that child. Tell her, "Your feelings are valid. You are important. I am here to listen to you now." This exercise signals safety to your nervous system. It helps you "re-parent" yourself. You stop looking for a partner to fill the void of your past because you are already filling it.

The Mirror Talk Practice

Standing in front of a mirror and looking into your own eyes is a powerful way to reaffirm your worth. Looking with kindness can reverse the pattern of turning away from yourself.

1. Stand in front of the mirror.
2. Look into your eyes for two minutes.
3. Say, "I see you. You matter. I am choosing you today."
4. List five things you love about your personality out loud. Do not mention your looks.

If this feels uncomfortable, it means your internal validation muscles are weak. Practice this every morning for seven days. Your brain will start to believe the words over time.

Implementing the N.A.N. Framework for Yourself

You can use Zach Mercurio's framework to provide the significance you crave. Do not wait for him to do it. Do it for yourself today.

1. Notice Yourself

Set a timer for three times a day. Ask, "What am I feeling right now?". Label the emotion without judgment. If you feel tired, rest. If you feel thirsty, drink. By noticing and meeting your own physical and emotional needs, you teach your brain that you are a priority.

2. Affirm Yourself

Celebrate your "quiet wins." Achieve something meaningful without telling anyone or posting it online. Feel the satisfaction of finishing a task or sticking to a habit. Allow yourself to feel pride. Track your progress in skills and alignment with your values rather than seeking applause.

3. Need Yourself

Remind yourself why you are indispensable to your own future. Write down your long-term goals. See how your current health and peace are necessary for you to reach them. You are the only person who will be with you for your whole life. You are your own most important partner.

The "Let Them" Shift for Being Unseen

The "Let Them" Theory by Mel Robbins is a tool for emotional independence. If he wants to ignore you, let him. If he wants to prioritize his friends over your plans, let him.

When you "let them," you stop wasting energy on things you cannot control. You stop trying to manage his behavior or "teach" him how to value you. You detach from the outcome. This reduces your stress and anxiety. You move from an external locus of control to an internal one. You reclaim the time you spent overthinking his silence and put it toward your own growth.

This is not about being passive. It is about choosing where your energy goes. If he does not see your value, that is a reflection of his limitations, not your worth. Stop trying to prove yourself to someone who is not looking. Reclaim your strength for your own path.

The Trap of the "Situationship" Facade

When we feel unseen, we often hide our real needs to stay "safe." We pretend we are okay with being casual. We tell ourselves that some attention is better than none. This is a facade that leads to unfulfilling "situationships."

Data from 2025 shows that 70% of daters feel that modern practices do not align with their actual needs. You want a bond, but you accept a "scroll." You hide your desire for commitment to avoid appearing "too much," but hiding your real self only wins you a prize that does not fit you.

A priority mindset requires "Truecasting." This means showing up as your real self from the start. You state your values. You share your goals. You do not wait for him to set the tone. If your real self does not get his approval, that is good data. It means he is not your person. It is better to be solo and authentic than partnered and invisible.

Reclaiming Your Relational Value

Your brain maintains an internal model of how much others value you. This is your "relational value." When you accept being an option, your brain recalibrates your perceived worth downward. You start to think that "crumbs" are all you deserve.

You can update this model through "Provisional Action." This means acting to generate information rather than to get a specific outcome. State a need and watch the response. If he ignores the need, you have your data. You do not need to wait for him to change. You can choose to walk away because you value your own peace more than his presence.

Healthy relationships are built on mutual respect and consistent effort. They require two people who are willing to be seen and heard. If you are the only one doing the emotional work, the relationship is one-sided. It is time to stop being the only person holding the bridge.

Practical Exercises for Internal Security

Use these drills to rewire your reward system and build a solid sense of self.

1. **The "Emotional Weather Report":** Every evening, describe your emotions as if they were a place or a type of weather. This helps you distance yourself from the pain and see it as temporary.
2. **The "Thought-on-Trial" Worksheet:** When you feel "not good enough," put that thought on the stand. Write down the evidence for it and against it using facts, not feelings. The verdict usually shows that your worth is independent of his opinion.
3. **Build a Comfort List:** List five activities that make you feel grounded and safe (e.g., a warm bath, a walk in nature, reading a book). When you feel unseen by him, turn to this list. Provide the comfort you need for yourself.
4. **Identify Your Non-Negotiables:** Write a list of five things you require in a partner. Consistency and respect should be at the top. If a man cannot meet these in the first month, he does not get a second one.

Conclusion: Living in the Light

True intimacy requires you to be visible. You cannot build a home with someone who treats you like a ghost. When you stop trying to force him to see you, you finally see the wide world around you. You realize that you are the prize. You do not need to prove your worth to a man who is too scared to see it.

The path to a priority relationship starts with choosing yourself first. You have the force of neuroplasticity on your side. You can learn new ways of thinking and being. You can rebuild your sense of self step by step.

Stop waiting for a text that only gives you crumbs. Start living a life that offers you everything you deserve. The forest of confusion is behind you. The field of clarity is open. Take the first step toward yourself today. You are seen. You are valued. You are the priority.

REFLECTION EXERCISES

CHAPTERS 5 TO 8

With these exercises, you will apply the science and tools from the recent chapters to your own life. These drills use techniques from Cognitive Behavioral Therapy (CBT), Dialectical Behavior Therapy (DBT), and somatic work. They help you rewire your brain and break the "option" cycle. Write your answers by hand in a journal. Data shows that hand-writing engages your motor cortex. This helps you process hard emotions better than typing.

Chapter 5: Link Past Wounds to Present Choices

Chapter 5 looked at the "age five blueprint." You learned how early bonds with parents create a map for love. These exercises help you see that map clearly. They give you the tools to stop following paths that lead to pain.

Exercise 5.1: The Mirror of Childhood Origins

Your brain uses a template for connection formed in early life. If care was sporadic, you hunt for love from people who withhold it. This exercise searches for the origins of your current behavior.

1. **Recall a Caregiver:** Think of the primary person who raised you. How did they respond when you cried or needed help? Were they consistent? Or were they busy, cold, or unpredictable?
2. **The Family Load:** Who in your family carried the emotional load? Who avoided it? How did that shape your view of what a partner should do?
3. **The Price of Love:** What did love "cost" you in your family? Did you have to be the peacemaker, the golden child, or the invisible one to get attention?
4. **Identify the Echo:** Look at the man you are currently chasing. In what ways does his behavior mirror that caregiver? Does he use the same type of silence? Does he offer the same type of vague praise?
5. **The Biological Recognition:** Write down three ways your current "chemistry" feels like your past home environment. Is it a "spark" of joy or a "spark" of familiar anxiety?

Exercise 5.2: The Familiarity Audit (Breaking the Chemistry Trap)

We are often drawn to what is emotionally familiar, even if it is not safe. People raised in unhealthy environments often confuse intimacy with uncertainty or unpredictability.

1. **The "Normal" List:** List five behaviors you consider "normal" in a relationship (e.g., waiting for texts, feeling unsure of your status, walking on eggshells).
2. **The Safety Check:** Are these behaviors actually healthy? If a friend told you her partner did these things, what would you say to her?
3. **The Evidence Table:** Create a table with two columns: "Anxiety-Driven Spark" and "Healthy Connection Data."
    - o In the first column, list things that make your heart race but leave you feeling insecure (e.g., "He texted me after three days").

    - In the second column, list concrete signs of reliability (e.g., "He planned a date four days in advance").
4. **The Shift:** Write a new list of what "safe" looks like. Use concrete words like "consistent," "planned," and "respectful." Read this list out loud every morning.

Exercise 5.3: The Vertical Arrow Drill for Core Beliefs

Use this Exercise CR9 from CBT to find the beliefs behind your dating choices.

1. **Identify a Trigger Thought:** Write down a recent thought you had when he ignored you (e.g., "He's probably talking to someone else").
2. **The Downward Inquiry:** Ask yourself: "If that is true, what does it mean about me?".
    - Answer: "It means I'm not interesting enough."
3. **Repeat the Question:** "If that's true, what does it mean about me?".
    - Answer: "It means I will never find someone who stays."
4. **Identify the Core Wound:** Keep going until you reach a fundamental belief (e.g., "I am fundamentally unlovable").
5. **The Logical Counter:** Write a fact-based response to that core wound. "My worth is a fact, not a result of his text habits. I am a whole person regardless of his choice."

Exercise 5.4: Redrawing the Path (Future Self-Visualization)

Healing starts with the act of choosing a new story. Use neuroplasticity to form new neural connections.

1. **The "Who Am I Becoming?" Prompt:** Write for 15 minutes about the version of you who only accepts priority treatment. Imagine yourself five years from now. What are you doing? Where are you living? How do you feel in your body?
2. **The Values Check-in:** Which three values do you want to be more visible in your life this year? (e.g., honesty, rest, clarity).
3. **The Inner Child Comfort Ritual:** Close your eyes. Imagine yourself as a five-year-old who felt ignored or unseen. Visualize your adult self kneeling down to embrace that child. Say: "I see you. You are a priority now. I will not ignore your needs".

4. **The Daily Choice:** List one action you will take today that aligns with your new map. This might be deleting a dating app for a day or calling a supportive friend.

Chapter 6: Watch Out for the Partner Who Builds High Walls

This section helps you identify the "fortress" partner. You will learn to trust the data of his actions over the hope of his potential.

Exercise 6.1: The Fortress Diagnostic

Wall-builders often have a history of short-term bonds or "situationships".

1. **The Relationship History Audit:** What do you know about his past? Does he blame all his exes for being "needy" or "crazy"? Does he avoid talking about depth?
2. **The Intellectualization Check:** When you bring up an emotion, does he respond with logic or facts? Does he analyze your feelings instead of feeling them?
3. **The Intimacy Hangover Log:** Does he go silent or pull away after a great, vulnerable date? Track the gaps in his communication for one week.
4. **The Reward System Data:** Scans show that dismissive avoidants have quiet reward circuits during closeness. Write this down: "I cannot change his biology with my effort. My love is not a cure for his wall."

Exercise 6.2: Identifying Physiological Flooding

Stonewalling is a sign that his body is in survival mode. His heart rate is likely over 100 beats per minute.

1. **Recall a Conflict:** Describe the last time he shut down or walked away. How did you react? Did you chase him or get louder?
2. **The Body Map:** Draw a simple outline of a body. Color in where you feel tension when he shuts down. Is it in your throat? Your chest?
3. **The Pursuit-Withdrawal Loop:** Notice how your chasing makes him run faster. Write down what happens when you stop chasing during a shutdown.

4. **The 20-Minute Rule Script:** Practice a script for next time. "I see that we are both overwhelmed. I'm going to take a break for 20 minutes to calm down. Let's talk again at".

Exercise 6.3: Behavioral Experiments for Availability

You can test for real interest early in a connection to save yourself time.

1. **The Vulnerability Test:** Share a small, real fear or a minor struggle today. Note his reaction. Did he offer empathy or a kind word? Or did he change the subject or give you a "fact"?
2. **The Needs Test (DEAR MAN):** State a clear requirement using the DBT tool.
   - **Describe:** "We only see each other on weeknights."
   - **Express:** "I feel like a side project when we don't have weekend dates."
   - **Assert:** "I want to go on a real date this Saturday afternoon."
   - **Reinforce:** "It would make me feel more secure in this connection."
3. **The Data Log:** Keep a list of "Green Flags" (consistent actions) and "Red Flags" (broken promises). Look at the list every Sunday to see the raw truth.

Exercise 6.4: The Potential vs. Reality Ledger

We often fall in love with a man's potential instead of his current reality.

1. **The "Dream Version":** List the traits he shows only once in a while. This is his potential.
2. **The "Daily Version":** List how he treats you on a regular Tuesday. This is his reality.
3. **The Service Zone Audit:** Are you in the "service zone"? Does he only call when he needs a favor, a hookup, or a listener? List the times he has served your needs without being asked.
4. **The Exit Cost:** Write down the cost of waiting for the "dream version" to stay permanently. How much of your life are you losing while you wait?

Chapter 7: Calm the Fear of Being Alone

This section looks at the "tribe" alarm in your head. You will learn to build a village so that you never date from a place of hunger.

Exercise 7.1: Identifying the Primal Alarm

Your brain treats being alone as a threat to your survival.

1. **Identify the Panic:** When you are home alone on a Saturday, what physical signs do you feel? A tight chest? A knot in your gut?
2. **The Anxiety Dialogue:** If your anxiety could speak, what would it say? (e.g., "You are forgotten," "You will always be alone").
3. **The Logical Update:** Tell your survival brain the facts: "I am safe. I have food, shelter, and water. A man's presence is a want, not a survival requirement".
4. **The Silence Audit:** Sit in a quiet room for ten minutes today with no phone. What thoughts come up? Label them as "old false alarms" or "current facts."

Exercise 7.2: The Positive Solitude Hierarchy

You can build your "solitude muscles" through gradual exposure therapy.

1. **Create Your Ladder:** Rank solo activities from 0 to 100 based on how much anxiety they cause you.
   - Example 20/100: Taking a 10-minute solo walk.
   - Example 50/100: Sitting in a coffee shop for 30 minutes without a phone.
   - Example 90/100: Going to a movie or dinner alone.
2. **The Weekly Challenge:** Pick one activity from the lower end of your ladder. Do it this week.
3. **The 50% Rule:** Stay in the activity until your anxiety drops by at least 50% from its peak. This teaches your brain that you can tolerate the distress.
4. **The Reflection:** How did your body feel after you finished? Did the "saber-toothed tiger" arrive? Record your victory.

Exercise 7.3: The Village Audit (Oxytocin Balancing)

Women with strong friendship networks report higher life satisfaction when single than when in poor relationships.

1. **List Your Tribe:** Write down five people who consistently show up for you. These can be friends, family, or mentors.
2. **The Mattering Check:** In these relationships, do you feel Noticed, Affirmed, and Needed?
3. **The Connection Deposit:** Schedule one "One-on-One Time" (Two-Time) with a friend this week.
4. **Rebalancing the Focus:** Are you putting 100% of your emotional needs on a "maybe" partner? Plan a "Three-Time" group event to remind your brain that you are part of a larger tribe.

Exercise 7.4: Reframing the Solo Narrative

Media often portrays solitude as a failure. You must build your own sanctuary.

1. **The Thought Record for Singleness:**
    - Situation: Seeing a couple in public.
    - Unhelpful Thought: "I'm a failure because I'm solo."
    - Evidence Against: List your professional wins, your deep friendships, and your skills.
2. **The Benefit List:** List five things you can *only* do well alone (e.g., reading without interruption, decorating your space exactly how you want).
3. **The Positive Reframe:** Write this and post it on your mirror: "I am solo so I can focus on my own growth. This is a sanctuary, not a sentence".

Chapter 8: Comfort the Part of You That Feels Unseen

This section focuses on the "mattering deficit." You will learn to provide your own validation and reclaim your identity.

Exercise 8.1: The Internal Mattering Audit (N.A.N.)

Zach Mercurio defines mattering as being Noticed, Affirmed, and Needed.

1. **The Relationship Scorecard:** In your current bond, on a scale of 1-10:
    - o How much do you feel truly heard?
    - o How much are your unique gifts affirmed?
    - o How much do you feel indispensable to his world?
2. **The Self-Mattering Drill:** How can you provide these for yourself today?
    - o **Notice:** Scan your body from toe to head. Express gratitude for each part and notice any tension.
    - o **Affirm:** List three things you did well today that no one saw. Do not tell anyone.
    - o **Need:** Remind yourself why you are essential to your own future. Write: "I need myself to be healthy so I can reach [Goal]."
3. **The Shift:** How would your life change if you stopped waiting for his gaze to feel real?

Exercise 8.2: Default Mode Network Reset (Reclaiming Identity)

Trauma can make you feel "invisible" or "like an object".

1. **Naming Emotions (Engaging the PFC):** When you feel unseen, say it out loud. "I feel invisible right now because he didn't reply." This moves the activity from your emotional brain to your logical brain.
2. **Interrupting the Rumination:** When you find yourself in a "what if" loop, stand up and move. Do a "TIPP" skill: Splash cold water on your face or do 20 jumping jacks.
3. **The "Who Am I?" Inventory:** Forget others' perspectives. Write a letter to your past self about who you are *now*. Include your strengths, your hobbies, and your favorite memories.
4. **Defining Non-Negotiables:** Create a list of clear "Deal-Breakers." These are behaviors that will cause you to leave immediately. If you have no boundaries, you have no identity.

Exercise 8.3: Shifting from Sugar to Nourishment

External validation is like a sugar rush. Internal validation is nourishment.

1. **The Daily Achievement Log:** Keep a record for three days. Every time you feel proud of yourself, write it down.
2. **The "Quiet Win" Practice:** Accomplish one task today (e.g., finishing a project, cleaning a space) and do not post it online. Sit for five minutes and feel the pride in your own body.
3. **The Thought-on-Trial Worksheet:** Put the thought "I only matter if he likes me" on the stand. Present the evidence for and against. Reach a verdict based on facts.
4. **Values Alignment Check:** Ask: "Did I live in alignment with my values today?". Even if it was messy, did you stay true to your boundaries?

Exercise 8.4: Mirror Talk and Reparenting

Looking into your own eyes with kindness can reverse the pattern of self-neglect.

1. **The Mirror Challenge:** Stand in front of a mirror. Look into your eyes for two minutes without looking away.
2. **The Compassionate Response:** If your inner critic speaks, replace those thoughts with: "I'm learning and growing. I am doing my best, and that is enough."
3. **The Direct Reaffirmation:** Say out loud: "I see you. You matter. I am choosing you today."
4. **The Self-Compassion Pause:** Place one hand on your chest and feel the warm sensation. Take three breaths and say: "May I be safe. May I be happy and at ease."

PART THREE

THE BIOLOGY OF THE BOND

CHAPTER 9

TRUST YOUR BODY TO SENSE DANGER

You walk into a restaurant to meet him. Your palms are slightly damp. You feel a strange fluttering in your stomach. You tell yourself it is just excitement. You think these are "butterflies" because you really like him. A few hours later, you feel a sharp headache. Your neck feels stiff and tight. Your body is trying to tell you something that your mind is not ready to hear. Your nervous system has detected a threat to your safety.

This chapter looks at the biological tools your body uses to sense relational danger. We examine how your brain and gut work together to keep you safe. We look at the latest data from 2025 and 2026 on somatic markers and neuroception. You will learn to tell the difference between healthy attraction and a survival response. You will find the tools to recalibrate your internal compass so you can trust your gut again.

The Sentinel System of the Body

Your nervous system is a high-speed tool for detecting risk. It scans your environment for cues of safety or danger every second. This process happens without you thinking about it. Scientists call this "neuroception." This evaluation happens deep in your brain before your conscious mind can form a single word.

For most of human history, being left out meant death. Our ancestors could not survive the wild alone. Because of this, the brain evolved to treat social rejection as a physical injury. When he treats you like an option, your body reacts as if you are in physical danger. This biological sentinel system uses the amygdala, the autonomic nervous system, and your gut to protect your life.

Why does your body react so strongly to a late-night text?. It is because your survival circuits view inconsistency as a fundamental threat. Your brain co-opted the neural pathways for physical pain to signal social loss. This is why being deprioritized "hurts" in a literal, physical way. It is not a mood. It is a survival signal.

The Anatomy of Relational Alarm

The detection of threat begins in the central extended amygdala. This is a network of brain regions that integrates fear and anxiety. It has two main parts. The central nucleus handles immediate threats. This is the part that fires when he snaps at you or withdraws suddenly. The second part, the bed nucleus of the stria terminalis (BST), handles uncertain or distant threats.

If your relationship is unstable, your BST stays active. You live in a state of chronic worry. You wonder where you stand. You analyze every word for a sign of trouble. This keeps your autonomic network engaged. It causes muscle tension, sleep issues, and that persistent "gut feeling" that something is wrong.

Recent studies show that the medial amygdala is very sensitive to social cues. If you feel like an option, this area becomes overactive. You start to "over-read" his facial expressions. You look for signs of rejection in his tone of voice. This narrows your "window of tolerance." Even small shifts in his mood feel like a total collapse of the bond.

Brain Region	Task in Relational Safety	Physical Sign
Central Nucleus	Immediate threat response	Rapid pulse; acute panic
Bed Nucleus (BST)	Chronic, uncertain threat	Constant worry; insomnia
Medial Amygdala	Processing social signals	Sensitivity to facial cues
Basolateral Amygdala	Linking memory to emotion	Scent/sound triggers of rejection

The Polyvagal Ladder of Safety

Stephen Porges developed the concept of neuroception to describe how we evaluate risk. When your system detects safety, it uses the ventral vagal complex. This supports connection, trust, and growth. If he gives you "mixed signals," your nervous system can never settle.

You get caught between warmth and withdrawal. This inconsistency prevents you from reaching a state of true safety. Instead, you stay in a state of sympathetic activation. This is the "fight or flight" mode. You might chase him for validation or feel constantly agitated. If the stress becomes too much, you might enter a "shutdown" or dorsal vagal state. This feels like numbness or being "spaced out."

Trauma from your past can bias your neuroception. It might make you sense threat in safe places. Or it might numb you to real danger if you grew up in chaos. Clinical tests like the Neuroception of Psychological Safety Scale (NPSS) now help measure this. If you score low on body sensations, you likely struggle to regulate your emotions in relationships.

The Social Pain Network

Your brain does not see a difference between a broken heart and a broken arm. Functional scans show that social rejection activates the same areas as physical injury. The primary regions are the dorsal anterior cingulate cortex (dACC) and the anterior insula. These handle the "distress" part of pain.

In one study, people viewed photos of an ex who had rejected them. Their brains showed activation in areas usually reserved for heat or physical burns. When you realize you are just an option, your brain processes it as a literal injury. This biological fact validates your agony.

Does this mean your feelings are "all in your head"?. No, they are represented in your whole body. One study even found that common pain relievers could reduce hurt feelings. This shows that the link between social loss and physical pain is deep and biological. Your body uses the pain system to warn you that you are losing your "tribe."

Somatic Markers: The Gut as a Map

Neuroscientist Antonio Damasio proposed the Somatic Marker Hypothesis. He argues that your body creates physiological "markers" to guide your choices. These are the "hunches" you feel before you even think. They are built from your past wins and losses.

In a relationship where you are an option, your body learns to associate certain behaviors with pain. You might feel a sting in your chest when he texts late at night. You might feel your stomach tighten when he cancels plans. These are somatic markers trying to bias you toward self-protection.

Learning from the "Bad Decks"

We can use the Iowa Gambling Task to see how this works. In this test, people pick from different decks of cards. Some decks offer high immediate gains but big long-term losses. Healthy people develop a "sweaty palm" response before picking from a bad deck. They feel the risk before they know it.

A man who love-bombs you but is inconsistent is a "bad deck." He offers high intensity (the high gain) but leads to long-term pain (the big loss). If your somatic markers are damaged by trauma, you might keep picking from the "bad deck" despite the warning signs. You ignore the gut feeling because you are chasing the initial high.

The Gut-Brain Axis and Intuition

The "gut feeling" is a real biological event. It is rooted in the gut-brain axis. This is a two-way link between your digestive tract and your brain. The vagus nerve is the main line for these signals. It sends data from your organs to your brainstem.

Your gut is often called your "second brain." It has over 100 million neurons. It produces 90% of your body's serotonin. When you sense relational danger, your brain sends signals that change your gut. This causes nausea, butterflies, or bloating.

Interoception is the process of sensing these internal signals. It is the foundation of your intuition. People who are good at this can sense a partner's lack of commitment early, but chronic stress can fragment this awareness. You might feel the nausea but suppress it to keep the bond. You must learn to listen to the data your gut is sending.

Mechanism	Path	Effect on Perception
Vagus Nerve	Neural	Direct sensing of "vibes" and comfort
Cytokine Signaling	Immune	Inflammation; "sickness behavior"
Microbial Metabolites	Biochemical	Influencing mood and dopamine levels
HPA Axis	Endocrine	Sustained cortisol; stress reactivity

High Sensitivity in the Dating World

About 20% of people are Highly Sensitive People (HSPs). Recent research from 2025 shows that HSPs are more prone to anxiety in bad environments, but they also respond better to help and good bonds.

The HSP brain shows more activity in areas for awareness and empathy. You "over-read" social cues. You pick up on subtle facial shifts or changes in tone. This makes you a great partner, but it also makes you the first to sense a "vibe shift."

For an HSP, being an option is very tiring. The ambiguity of a non-committal man creates a "mental cage" of worry. Your system is finely tuned. It is easily thrown off by relational toxins. You need to recognize that your sensitivity is a gift for detecting danger. It is not "weakness." It is a high-speed radar system for your heart.

Clinical Red Flags for 2026

Dating in 2026 is often digital and shallow. This leads to "analog anxiety." We fear face-to-face chemistry after years of screens. Your body may register certain red flags during the dating phase.

1. **Surveillance:** You feel watched rather than cared for.
2. **Possession:** He tries to "own" your time or your thoughts.
3. **Defensiveness:** Every concern you raise is met with an attack.
4. **Invalidation:** You are frequently made to feel "crazy."
5. **Unsafe Talk:** You feel you cannot speak your mind without a fight.

"Love Bombing" is another major flag. He gives you intense affection that turns hot and cold. Your body might feel this as "electricity," but it is often the precursor to a collapse. A priority partner will not rush the bond. He will offer consistency and clarity.

The Cost of Ignoring Your Body

Chronic relational stress has a high price. When you stay an option, your body stays in "defense mode." Your HPA axis stays active. This keeps cortisol flowing through your system.

Short-term stress is okay, but chronic cortisol harms your organs. It can cause shrinkage in the brain areas for memory and fear. You might experience "brain fog" or poor decision-making. Your body keeps the score of every time you ignore your gut.

Body System	Stress Result	Clinical Signs
Neurological	Brain atrophy	Memory loss; brain fog
Endocrine	HPA dysregulation	Weight gain; chronic fatigue

Body System	Stress Result	Clinical Signs
Cardiovascular	Sympathetic surge	High blood pressure; racing heart
Gastrointestinal	Microbiome shifts	Stomach knots; IBS flare-ups
Reproductive	Hormone suppression	Irregular periods; low libido

Distinguishing Trauma from Intuition

It is hard to trust your gut if you have been hurt before. Trauma rearranges your wiring. It can be easy to mistake a trauma response for intuition.

Intuition is a quiet, calm knowing. It is rooted in the present. Trauma responses are loud and urgent. They involve physiological "flooding." Your heart races and your palms sweat. Trauma is an echo of the past. Intuition is a signal for the now.

Learning the difference takes practice. Trauma feels like being "hit" by a wave. Intuition feels like a solid ground. You can use grounding tools to clear the static. When your body is calm, your intuitive signal becomes clear.

Rebuilding Your Somatic Safety

Recalibrating your system requires body-based work. Talk therapy is often not enough because trauma lives in the body. You must teach your nervous system that the "emergency" is over.

Vagus Nerve Drills

The vagus nerve is your body's source of calm. You can stimulate it to move out of "fight or flight."

- **Voo Sounding:** Take a deep breath. Exhale with a long "vooooo" sound. The vibration stimulates the nerve.
- **Box Breathing:** Inhale for four counts. Hold for four. Exhale for four. Hold for four. This calms your flight response.

- **Cold Water:** Splash cold water on your face for 10 seconds. This triggers a reset of your nervous system.
- **Humming:** Simple humming stimulates the throat muscles that link to the vagus nerve.

Grounding Exercises

These tools anchor you in the present moment. They break the loop of worry.

- **The 5-4-3-2-1 Drill:** Identify 5 things you see, 4 you can touch, 3 you hear, 2 you smell, and 1 you taste.
- **Orienting:** Slowly look around the room. Let your eyes land on something pleasant, like a plant. This signals safety to your brain.
- **The Butterfly Hug:** Cross your arms and tap each shoulder in a rhythm. This soothes your amygdala.
- **Shake It Out:** Gently shake your hands and arms for one minute. This releases trapped stress energy.

The Integrated Relational Compass

Sensing danger is not a flaw. It is a gift. Our culture often prizes "coolness" or detachment. If you feel unsafe, people might call you "needy." However, science shows that consistency and safety are biological needs.

When you feel safe, your body can rest and heal. When you are an option, your body is in an expensive state of defense. Breaking the pattern is not about "thinking" your way out. It is about feeling your way into the truth.

By trusting your racing heart and your sinking gut, you take back your power. You stop being a responder to his crumbs. You become the creator of your own peace. When you honor your body's signals, you find the strength to choose partners who offer real safety. You stop being an option the moment you listen to your own biological truth.

Scientific Note on Vagal Tone Vagal tone is measured through Heart Rate Variability (HRV). Higher variability shows that your heart can adapt to stress. Research in 2025 confirms that high HRV is linked to better emotional control. In toxic relationships, vagal tone is often suppressed.

Strengthening your tone through breathing and movement helps you stay calm when a partner is inconsistent. It allows you to make better choices for your own well-being.

CHAPTER 10

HEAL THE BRAIN AFTER A BAD BREAKUP

You feel as though a part of your body is missing. Your chest aches. Your breath comes in short, ragged bursts. You look at your phone every few minutes. You hope for a name that no longer appears. You tell yourself to "just get over it," but your body refuses to listen. This is not just a heavy heart. It is a biological crisis. Recent findings from 2025 and 2026 show that heartbreak is a state of physical withdrawal. Your brain is not just sad; it is in panic mode.

This chapter looks at the science of the recovery process. We look at the facts of how your brain rewires after loss. You will learn how to stabilize your nervous system and quiet the mental noise. We provide tools to help you move from a state of chemical detox to a life of autonomy. You can heal because your brain is plastic. You can form new paths that no longer lead back to him.

The Chemistry of the Crash

When you are in a relationship, your brain is a factory for "happy chemicals." You get a steady supply of dopamine, oxytocin, and vasopressin. These chemicals bond you to your partner. They create a sense of safety and joy. When the bond ends, the factory shuts down. You experience a massive neurochemical crash.

This crash is similar to quitting a powerful drug. Your mesolimbic reward system enters a state of detox. The ventral tegmental area (VTA) sends out distress signals. It scans your life for the "lost reward." This is why you replay old voice notes or check his Instagram. Your brain is trying to get a "hit" of emotional dopamine to stop the pain.

At the same time, your serotonin levels drop. Dopamine and serotonin compete for the same resources in your body. When your brain is hunting for dopamine, it makes less serotonin. This drop causes the obsessive thoughts and high anxiety you feel. You are not "crazy" or "weak." You are managing a chemical imbalance that takes time to level out.

Neurochemical	Function Before Loss	State After Loss	Physical Result
Dopamine	Drives joy and motivation	Severe crash; seeking "fix"	Lethargy; obsession with texts
Oxytocin	Builds trust and security	Sharp drop; loss of buffer	Intense loneliness; chest pain
Serotonin	Stabilizes mood and sleep	Marked reduction	Ruminating loops; volatility
Cortisol	Handles short-term stress	Chronic elevation	Fatigue; weakened immunity

The Physicality of the Social Wound

Your brain does not see a gap between a broken bone and a broken heart. Scans from 2025 show that social rejection uses the same hardware as physical injury. The dorsal anterior cingulate cortex (dACC) and the anterior insula (AI) handle the "distress" part of pain. When he stops choosing you, these areas flare up. They send a signal that your survival is at risk.

This overlap explains why you feel "punched in the gut" or "aching." Your brain co-opted the pain system over millions of years of evolution. For our ancestors, being alone meant certain death. Rejection acted as an alarm to get back to the tribe. Today, that alarm goes off when a connection dies. It is a loud, inescapable signal meant to grab your attention.

A specific feature of social pain is that you can "relive" it. If you break an arm, the pain stops once it heals. If you think about a rejection from three months ago, your dACC can activate again. This happens because the prefrontal cortex analyzes the loss. It keeps the wound fresh. To heal, you must stop the analysis and start the stabilization.

The Ruminative Trap: The Default Mode Network

You find yourself in a loop. You ask "What if?" or "Why me?" a thousand times a day. You are caught in the "brooding" response. This is driven by the Default Mode Network (DMN). This is a set of brain areas that stay active when you are not focused on a task.

In a healthy brain, the DMN helps you reflect on your life, but after a breakup, it becomes hyper-connected. It builds a narrative of nostalgia and fantasy. You stop seeing the reality of how he treated you. Instead, you see a highlight reel of the "good times." This network also works to keep memories stable. By thinking about him constantly, you are training your brain not to forget.

This hyper-active DMN pulls resources away from your "Task-Positive Network" (TPN). This is why you cannot focus at work or finish simple chores. Your brain is so busy with its internal story that it lacks the energy for the external world. Breaking the cycle requires you to silence the DMN through action and focus.

The Algorithm of Obsession: Reward Prediction Error

Why is it so hard to stop checking his social media? The answer lies in Reward Prediction Error (RPE). This is the difference between what you expect to happen and what actually happens.

When you check his profile, you expect to feel nothing or feel hurt. But if you see a post that makes you feel "connected" for a second, you get a massive dopamine surge. This is a "Positive Prediction Error." It acts as a powerful teaching signal. It tells your brain: "Checking this profile works! Do it again!".

Your brain also updates its baseline. The "hit" you got today will not be enough tomorrow. You will need more frequent updates or more personal data to get the same relief. This creates a cycle that mirrors addiction. Even a small "crumb" of digital data can make you ignore the high emotional cost of the bond. You become a risk-seeker, reaching out when you know you should stay silent.

RPE State	Mathematical Formula	Brain Action	Behavioral Outcome
Positive	Get > Expect	Dopamine burst	Intense urge to stalk social media
Negative	Get < Expect	Dopamine pause	Severe distress; desperation
Zero	Get = Expect	Baseline activity	Habituation; eventually leads to peace

The Systemic Toll: HPA Axis Dysregulation

Heartbreak is a total-body stressor. Your Hypothalamic-Pituitary-Adrenal (HPA) axis goes into overdrive. This triggers a massive release of cortisol. In a healthy state, cortisol drops once a threat is gone, but a bad breakup can create "glucocorticoid resistance." Your system stays in a state of high alert.

This constant stress can cause physical changes. Research from 2025 indicates that long-term stress can increase the mass of your adrenal glands. This locks you into a hyper-responsive state. Even after he is gone, your body stays jumpy and tired. This tissue change takes weeks or months to reverse. You cannot force your way out of this; you must allow your body the time to cycle through its biological recovery.

Sleep loss makes this worse. Sleep usually inhibits the HPA axis, but heartbreak causes insomnia. This creates a "vicious cycle" where exhaustion fuels stress and stress prevents sleep. Data from the Endocrine Society suggests that oxytocin is a buffer for this. Women with high oxytocin levels before sleep loss show better moods the next day. Building non-romantic bonds can help protect your brain during this phase.

Neuroplasticity Protocols: How to Reset

You are not stuck with the "heartbroken brain." You can use the mechanics of neuroplasticity to rebuild your life. Two main processes help you detach: extinction and reconsolidation.

1. Extinction Learning

This is the process of creating a new, "safe" narrative. If seeing his name on a screen triggers a panic attack, you need "Exposure." You repeatedly encounter the cue without the reward (the text) or the pain (the fight). This creates a new neural path that competes with the old attachment memory. To make this stick, you must actively retrieve the "new" safety feeling rather than just avoiding him.

2. Memory Reconsolidation

This is the way to permanently change the emotional charge of a memory. Every time you recall a memory, it becomes temporary unstable. You have a "window" of about four hours to update it.

A 2025 protocol involves three steps:

1. **Reactivation:** Briefly think of a painful memory.
2. **Mismatch:** Introduce an experience that contradicts the memory. For example, visit the park where you fought, but go there with friends who make you laugh.
3. **Erasure:** This "prediction error" rewrites the emotional learning. You still remember what happened, but it no longer triggers the intense pain.

Stage	Duration	Neural Path
Reactivation	Minutes	Amygdala activation
Short-Term Shift	~30 min	Prefrontal control
Restabilization	~6 hours	Synaptic transition
Long-Term Reset	~24 hours	Synaptic restructuring

Clinical Modalities for Stabilization

Therapists in 2026 use structured methods to help you manage abandonment panic and emotional instability.

Triangle Therapy (TTB)

Triangle Therapy uses three modules to teach your body that you are safe alone.

- **Silence Module:** You sit in structured silence with a professional. This trains your vagus nerve to stay calm when there is a "pause" in connection.
- **Sound Module:** You use calibrated tones to regulate your stress response. This helps you stay calm during future arguments or high-stress talks.
- **Isolation Module:** You spend timed periods alone in a safe place. This helps you view solitude as "manageable" rather than "annihilation."

The PORT Model

Presence-Oriented Relationship Therapy focuses on the "neural configuration" of the individual. It uses "presence" to intervene in emotional loops and rebuild your sense of self after a betrayal. This model helps you move out of a survival cycle and into a state of comfort and security.

Lifestyle Strategies for Recovery

Because the loss affects your whole body, you must stabilize your physiology to heal your mind.

1. **Morning Sunlight:** Expose your eyes to early light. This regulates your cortisol cycle and helps you sleep.
2. **Daily Movement:** Exercise facilitates the recovery of the HPA axis. It reduces heightened cortisol responses, especially if you are prone to rumination.
3. **Hydrotherapy:** End your shower with 30 seconds of cold water. This energizes your system and clears the "emotional fog."
4. **Micro-Task Stacking:** Focus on "small wins." Making your bed or taking a five-minute walk triggers sustainable dopamine. This rebuilds your reward system without overwhelming it.
5. **Non-Romantic Bonds:** Spend ten minutes a day with a friend or family member. This builds oxytocin and helps reset your attachment circuits.

Conclusion: The Path to Autonomy

The pain of heartbreak is the engine of change. It serves as a catalyst for neural reorganization. You are dismantling a dependency and growing new pathways. You are moving away from needing a single person for stability.

By grasping that your recovery is governed by cellular timelines and chemical competition, you can stop blaming yourself. This is a biological detox. You have the ability to rewire your response to stress and rebuild your sense of self. You stop being an option when you provide your own internal rewards. Choose your peace. Choose your path. Choose yourself today.

CHAPTER 11

USE YOUR BREATH TO QUIET THE PANIC

You sit on the edge of your bed. Your heart hammers against your ribs like a trapped bird. Your phone lies face down, but you feel its presence like a hot coal. He hasn't replied to your text for six hours. You feel a familiar, cold wave of panic wash over you. Your chest feels tight. Your breath is shallow and fast. This is not just "worry." It is a full-body stress response. Your nervous system has detected a threat to your social safety. It has activated the same circuits that would help you run from a physical predator.

This chapter looks at the science of the panic response. We look at the facts of how your breath acts as a remote control for your brain. You will learn to use your own biology to silence the alarm. We examine the latest data from 2026 on neuroaffective interventions. You will find the tools to move from a state of "annihilation panic" to a state of calm security. You can regain control because your breath is the bridge between your body and your mind.

The Biological Alarm of the Unchosen

When you feel like an option, your brain stays in a state of high alert. This is called "threat vigilance." Your central extended amygdala integrations fear and anxiety data to keep you alive. The central nucleus (Ce) handles immediate threats, like a sharp word. The bed nucleus of the stria terminalis (BST) handles the chronic, uncertain threats of an unstable bond.

If a partner is inconsistent, your BST stays active. This sustained activity keeps your heart rate high and your muscles tense. You live in a mental cage of "what if" scenarios. This is a survival signal. In 2026, researchers have found that people with a history of neglect show even higher sensitivity in these regions. Their nervous systems are calibrated to detect rejection before it even happens.

This panic is a biological error. Your brain co-opted the physical pain system to alert you to social loss. Being ignored by him lights up your dorsal anterior cingulate cortex (dACC). This is the center for the "affective" component of pain, the part that makes a sensation feel distressing. When your heart aches, it is a real neurological event. Your body is trying to "scream" for connection to restore its sense of safety.

Moving Down the Polyvagal Ladder

Stephen Porges' Polyvagal Theory explains how your body evaluates safety. This happens through "neuroception," an automatic scan of your environment. Your nervous system operates in three main states.

1. **Ventral Vagal (The Green Zone):** You feel safe, calm, and connected. Your heart rate is steady. You can think clearly. This is where real intimacy lives.
2. **Sympathetic (The Yellow Zone):** You feel the "fight or flight" surge. This is the panic you feel when he goes silent. You want to text him fifty times. Your body is ready for battle.
3. **Dorsal Vagal (The Red Zone):** You feel numb, cold, or "spaced out." This is the shutdown that happens when the stress is too much. You give up. You feel invisible.

State	Autonomic Driver	Relational Sign
Ventral Vagal	Parasympathetic	Trust; clarity; priority
Sympathetic	Fight or Flight	Panic; chasing; anxiety
Dorsal Vagal	Shutdown	Numbness; withdrawal; silence

The uncertainty of being an option keeps you trapped between the Sympathetic and Dorsal zones. You never reach the peace of the Ventral zone because the cues of safety are missing. A 2026 study found that psychological safety is not just the absence of threat. It is a specific biological state that supports growth and repair. To heal, you must learn to manually shift your system back to the green zone.

The Breath as the Brake System

Your breath is the only part of your autonomic nervous system that you can control. When you are in a panic, you take short, shallow inhales. This tells your brain that you are in a "hostage negotiation" or a fight. It keeps the stress chemicals flowing.

To quiet the panic, you must change the signal. A longer exhale activates the vagus nerve. This nerve is the "vagus brake." It carries a message of calm from your lungs and heart to your brainstem. When you slow your breath, you are essentially telling your amygdala, "The emergency is over. You can stand down."

Recent clinical findings from 2025 show that just ten minutes of deep belly breathing can shift your cortisol levels. This shift allows your prefrontal cortex, the part of the brain that handles logic, to come back "online." When you are calm, you can see his inconsistency as data about *him*, not a verdict on *you*. You move from "Emotion Mind" to "Wise Mind."

The 2026 Triangle Therapy Protocol

In February 2026, a new neuroaffective intervention called Triangle Therapy (TTB) was detailed. This intervention uses three modules to teach your body that historically "catastrophic" environments are survivable. This is a somatic-first approach to healing attachment wounds.

1. The Silence Module

This module addresses the "annihilation panic" of being ignored. In TTB, individuals sit in structured silence for 5 to 50 minutes. This trains the ventral vagal complex to stay engaged even when there are no external cues. You learn that silence does not mean you have ceased to exist. You learn that the "pause" in connection is not a death sentence.

2. The Sound Module

Arguments often trigger a panic response. TTB uses calibrated auditory tones, starting at 400 Hz and 40 dB. The goal is to recalibrate your sympathetic response to intense sounds. This helps future disagreements remain "discussions" rather than escalating into perceived attacks. You learn to stay grounded while things are "noisy" around you.

3. The Isolation Module

The fear of being alone is the main anchor that keeps you as an option. TTB uses timed periods of isolation to re-encode aloneness as "tolerable solitude." It widens your "window of tolerance." This reduces compulsive contact-seeking. You learn that you are a safe person to be with, even when no one else is there.

Somatic Anchor Drills for Real Life

You do not need a clinic to start this work. You can use specific somatic drills to ground yourself the next time he leaves you on "read." These tools break the cycle of dissociation and hypervigilance.

The Voo Sound Toning

Inhale deeply into your belly. On the exhale, make a long, low "voooooo" sound. Feel the vibration in your chest and abdomen. This vibration directly stimulates the vagus nerve. It releases muscle tension and engages your parasympathetic system. Repeat this for five rounds to reset your nervous system.

The Cold Water Reset

If your panic is intense, use the "Dive Reflex." Splash ice-cold water on your face for 10 seconds. This triggers a rapid drop in heart rate. It is a physical override for your fight-or-flight response. It clears the "emotional fog" and brings you back to the present moment.

The Butterfly Hug

Cross your arms over your chest. Rest your hands on your opposite shoulders. Gently tap each hand alternately, left, right, left, right. Breathe slowly while you tap. This bilateral stimulation soothes the amygdala. It provides a sense of internal safety and containment.

The 5-4-3-2-1 Sensory Scan

When your mind is racing with "what if" thoughts, look away from your screen. Identify:

- 5 things you see.
- 4 things you can touch.
- 3 things you hear.
- 2 things you smell.
- 1 thing you taste. This drill anchors you in physical reality. It breaks the loop of the hyper-connected Default Mode Network (DMN).

Building Vagal Tone for Resilience

Vagal tone is measured through Heart Rate Variability (HRV). Higher variability means your heart can adapt to stress quickly. Low vagal tone is linked to being emotionally unstable and prone to anxiety. Research from 2025 shows that psychological resilience is positively correlated with a strong vagal tone.

Training your body to calm down after a stressor is a skill. Each time you use a breathing exercise or a somatic drill, you are "toning" your nerve. You are building a stronger physiological capacity to cope with his inconsistency.

A person with high vagal tone does not crumble when a partner is distant. They can tolerate the distress, look at the evidence, and make a logical choice. They realize that their worth is a fact, not a result of a partner's mood. When your body is stable, you stop being an option because you no longer need the "fix" of his attention to feel whole.

Distinguishing Trauma from True Intuition

One of the hardest parts of healing is learning to trust your gut again. Trauma often disguises itself as "intuition", but they feel different in the body.

- **Trauma Response:** Feels loud, urgent, and frantic. Your heart races. Your palms sweat. You feel like you *must* act now. It is an echo of a past wound.
- **True Intuition:** Feels quiet, calm, and solid. It is a "felt sense" in your gut or heart. It often comes with a sense of "knowing" that remains steady even when your mind is busy.

To find your true intuition, you must first clear the static of panic. Use your breath to move into a Ventral Vagal state. When your body is calm, ask yourself: "Is this connection making me feel energized or drained?". Trust the answer that comes from a settled nervous system.

Conclusion: Reclaiming Your Internal Compass

Your panic is a messenger, not a master. It is telling you that your environment is currently inconsistent. By using your breath and somatic tools, you regain the power to choose your response. You move from a reactive state to a proactive one.

You stop being an option the moment you prioritize your own biological peace. You no longer have to wait for a text to tell your body it is safe to rest. You provide that safety for yourself. When you are no longer a slave to the "ping" of his attention, you become free to choose partners who value you as their first priority. Your breath is the first step toward that freedom. Take a deep inhale now. Exhale slowly. You are in control.

Scientific Note on the "Dive Reflex"

Splashing cold water on the face stimulates the trigeminal nerve. This sends a signal to the vagus nerve to rapidly slow the heart. This is an ancient biological mechanism seen in all mammals. In moments of high relational distress, it acts as a "hard reset" for the autonomic nervous system. It is one of the most effective ways to break a panic attack or a ruminative loop.

CHAPTER 12

UNPLUG TO RESET YOUR REWARD SYSTEM

You reach for your phone before your eyes are even fully open. You scroll through his social media feed to see what time he was last active. You check the "seen" receipts on your latest message. You are looking for a sign that you are on his mind. This habit feels like a reflex. It feels like you are just being thorough or careful, but deep in your brain, a different process is taking hold. You are caught in a dopamine loop. You are using your screen to manage a chemical hunger. This behavior is not just a habit. It is a biological capture.

This chapter looks at the facts of digital addiction and relational "fix-seeking." We look at the science of why your phone makes it impossible to leave an unavailable man. You will learn how continuous scrolling changes your brain's reward hardware. We examine the latest data from 2025 and 2026 on receptor restoration. You will find a step-by-step protocol to reset your reward system. You can break the cycle because your brain has the force of neuroplasticity. You can teach your system to value real connection over a digital crumb.

The Neurochemistry of "The Hook"

Your brain is designed to seek rewards. For our ancestors, these rewards were food, water, and social safety. When you found something good, your brain released dopamine. This chemical is not about pleasure. It is about motivation. It is the "get up and go" chemical. It tells your brain that a specific action is worth doing again.

In a healthy relationship, dopamine release is steady and earned. Digital dating changes the math. Every ping, notification, or "like" triggers a small dopamine spike. Modern apps are built using "variable ratio reinforcement." This is the same logic used in slot machines. You do not know when the reward is coming. You do not know if the next swipe will be a match or if the next refresh will show a text. This uncertainty is what makes the behavior addictive.

When you receive a reward that is better than you expected, you get a massive surge. Scientists call this a "Positive Reward Prediction Error" (RPE). If you check his profile with low hopes and see he liked your photo, your brain gets a huge chemical hit. This surge directs your future behavior. It tells your brain to check the phone again and again to find that same high.

The Mechanism of Anhedonia

Your brain has a built-in defense against overstimulation. If you receive too many dopamine spikes, your brain starts to protect itself. It decreases the number of available dopamine receptors, specifically the D2 receptors. This is called "downregulation."

Think of it like a room with a very loud stereo. At first, the noise is overwhelming. To protect your hearing, you put on earplugs. Now, the music is at a safe level, but there is a cost. Because you have earplugs in, you can no longer hear the quiet sounds. You cannot hear a whisper or the wind in the trees.

In your brain, this manifests as anhedonia. This is a state where everyday activities seem dull. A conversation with a friend or a beautiful sunset no longer satisfies you. They do not reach the high dopamine threshold that your screen has set. You become a slave to the "artificial high" of his texts and "likes." You stay in the "option" cycle because everything else in your life feels "gray." You are not chasing him; you are chasing the only thing that still makes you feel alive.

The Failure of the "Braking System"

Digital addiction also weakens your Prefrontal Cortex (PFC). This is the part of your brain responsible for logic, impulse control, and decision-making. It acts as the "braking system" for your emotional impulses.

When you are constantly multitasking and switching between apps, your PFC becomes fatigued. You lose the ability to say "no" to the urge to check on him. Your working memory becomes less effective. You stop thinking about your long-term goals. You focus only on the immediate relief of the dopamine hit.

This creates a state of "digital captivity." Your ancestral brain is trapped in an algorithmic maze. Your choices become reflexes. You feel like you cannot stop yourself from checking your phone, even when you know it will hurt you. To reclaim your role as a priority, you must first reclaim your brain's ability to choose.

Brain System	Impact of Digital Overuse	Result for the "Option" Cycle
Reward Circuit	Receptor downregulation	Anhedonia; everyday life feels boring
Prefrontal Cortex	Weakened executive function	Inability to control impulses or leave him
Amygdala	Heightened threat detection	Anxiety and overthinking digital silence
GABA System	Chemical inhibition	Feeling "wired" and unable to rest

The 72-Hour Brain Reset

Emerging research from 2025 and 2026 shows that a short, intentional break can begin to rewire your reward circuitry. Taking a 72-hour break from your smartphone can change how dopamine acts in your brain. This is not about willpower. It is about allowing your biology to recalibrate.

Stage A: The Sensory Reset (Days 1-2)

In the first 48 hours, you will feel uncomfortable. This is the "detox" core. Your brain is used to 63 or more dopamine spikes every day from your phone. When those spikes stop, you will feel restless, empty, and bored. You might experience "phantom vibrations" where you think your phone is buzzing when it isn't.

This discomfort is a sign that your brain is beginning to repair its signaling paths. Stay the course. Use this time to engage in "analog" activities. Walk in a park. Cook a meal from a physical book. Have a face-to-face talk with a friend. These activities provide "low-arousal" rewards that help your receptors begin to upregulate.

Stage B: Neuroplastic Re-calibration (Days 3-10)

Between day three and day ten, your brain begins to increase the density of your dopamine and serotonin receptors. Your Prefrontal Cortex starts to re-engage. You will notice that your attention span gets longer. You feel more in control of your impulses.

During this stage, your levels of GABA, your brain's natural "calm down" chemical, begin to rise. The "wired" feeling starts to fade. You find that you can sit in silence without feeling a sense of panic. This is the foundation of emotional independence. You no longer need his digital "ping" to tell your body it is safe to rest.

Stage C: Circadian Rhythm Correction

The blue light from your screen suppresses the production of melatonin in your pineal gland. This disrupts your sleep and keeps your stress hormones high. Without evening screen exposure, your system resets. Melatonin levels begin to rise two to three hours earlier. Your sleep architecture improves, leading to deeper recovery. Better sleep means better brain health and a stronger "braking system" for your dating choices.

Practical Strategies for Digital Wellness

Taking back your digital wellness is not about giving up technology. It is about moving from passive use to intentional use. Use these strategies to protect your reward system from being hijacked.

1. **The "Greyscale" Hack:** Make your phone screen black and white. Vibrant icons are designed to stimulate your reward center. When the screen is gray, your brain finds the phone less interesting. This reduces the dopamine pull of the device.
2. **"Nuclear" Notifications:** Turn off every notification that is not from a real human being. Stop letting apps tell you when to look at your screen. This breaks the cue-action-reward cycle and puts you back in control of your time.
3. **Phone-Free Zones:** Keep the bedroom and the dining table "analog." Use a traditional alarm clock so you can avoid the "morning scroll." This allows your brain to start the day with focus rather than a reactive dopamine chase.
4. **The "Let Them" Theory:** Mel Robbins suggests using two words to reclaim your energy: "Let them." If he wants to ignore your text, let him. If he wants to be inconsistent, let him. You stop trying to manage his behavior through your screen. You focus on your own actions instead.
5. **Time-Box Your Swiping:** If you use dating apps, set a strict limit. Swipe for only 20 minutes a day, perhaps twice a week. This prevents the "illusion of choice" from overwhelming your brain and causing burnout.

Filling the Reward Gap

When you remove the high-stimulation rewards of your phone, you must replace them with something else. If you just leave a void, you will eventually relapse into the dopamine loop.

Look for activities that trigger "flow states." This is a state of complete immersion in a task. It happens when you are challenged but have the skills to meet the challenge. Flow suppresses the hyper-active Default Mode Network (DMN) and enhances the Executive Control Network (ECN). This provides emotional stability and reduces negative affect.

Try a creative pursuit, physical movement, or learning a new skill. These activities provide long-term satisfaction rather than a quick spike. They teach your brain that joy exists beyond the validation of one person. You move from being a consumer of his crumbs to being the creator of your own rewarding life.

Conclusion: Reclaiming Your Agency

Your reward system is a precious resource. It is meant to guide you toward things that support your life and growth. When you allow an unavailable man and a glowing screen to control it, you lose your agency. You become a passenger in your own life.

By unplugging, you allow your brain to heal. You allow your receptors to recover and your "braking system" to strengthen. You gain the mental clarity to see his behavior for what it is: a series of low-value signals that do not match your worth.

You stop being an option the moment you realize that your internal peace is worth more than any digital "hit." You do not need a notification to tell you that you are valuable. You provide your own validation through your actions and your values. Take back your "digital wellness" today. Put down the phone. Look at the real world. You are the pilot now.

Scientific Note on Dopamine vs. Pleasure

Dopamine is often called the "pleasure chemical," but this is a sensory processing error. Dopamine is about craving and motivation. Many other chemicals, like endorphins and opioids, handle the actual feeling of "liking." This means that chasing the dopamine hit of a text will never lead to lasting happiness. It only leads to a cycle of wanting more. Lasting satisfaction comes from activities that build serotonin and oxytocin through consistency and real-world connection.

REFLECTION EXERCISES

CHAPTERS 9 TO 12

These exercises help you move from theory into physical action. You will apply the science of your nervous system to your daily life. Use these drills to rewire your response to stress and reset your brain's reward system. Write your answers by hand in a journal. Data from 2025 shows that hand-writing engages your motor cortex. This helps you process hard emotions better than typing.

Chapter 9: Trust Your Body

Chapter 9 looked at how your body evaluates risk before you think. This process is called neuroception. These drills help you tune in to your internal alarm. You will learn to tell the difference between healthy interest and a survival response.

Exercise 9.1: The Interoceptive Baseline

Interoception is the ability to detect signals from inside your body. People who have been options for too long often lose this link. This drill restores it. 2025 research shows that interoceptive accuracy helps you navigate social risks with more clarity.

1. **Find a quiet space.** Sit with your feet flat on the floor. Close your eyes.
2. **Scan your body from toes to head.** Notice areas of heat, cold, tension, or ease.
3. **Label the sensations.** Use simple words like "tight," "buzzy," "heavy," or "light." Do not judge them. Just name them.
4. **Identify your "Safe Signal."** When do you feel most calm? Is it when you are reading? Is it when you are with a specific friend? Write down how your body feels in that moment. This is your "ventral vagal" baseline.
5. **The Somatic Match:** Think of a recent interaction with the man who treats you like an option. Does your body feel "wired" or "settled"? If you feel a "buzz" or a "tightness," your body is signaling a threat.

Exercise 9.2: The "Bad Deck" Audit

The Iowa Gambling Task is a tool used to study how the body senses risk. Participants choose from "advantageous" or "disadvantageous" decks. Healthy people develop a "sweaty palm" response before picking from a bad deck. They feel the risk before they know it.

1. **List his "High Immediate Gains."** What are the intense, passionate moments that keep you coming back? (e.g., intense texting, love bombing).
2. **List the "Long-Term Losses."** What is the price you pay for those moments? (e.g., days of silence, cancelled plans, feeling unimportant).
3. **The Body's Response:** How does your body feel *just before* you check your phone for his name? Note any stomach knots or shallow breathing. These are your "somatic markers." They are warning you about a "bad deck."
4. **The Decision:** Write this sentence: "I am ignoring my internal markers to chase a short-term high. I choose to prioritize my long-term safety instead."

Exercise 9.3: The Baylor Red Flag Screening

Psychiatrists at the Baylor College of Medicine defined red flags as actions that violate your identity. Use this checklist to audit your current connection.

- **Surveillance:** Do you feel monitored instead of cared for?
- **Defensiveness:** Does he attack when you raise a concern?
- **Invalidation:** Does he call you "crazy" or "too much"?
- **Love Bombing:** Did he start very intense and then turn cold?
- **Lack of Support:** Does he have real friends, or just "work colleagues"?

The Reflection: Pick the flag that your body reacts to most strongly. Where do you feel that reaction? (e.g., a pit in your stomach). Write this: "My body is sensing a violation of my values. I will honor this signal."

Exercise 9.4: The 5-4-3-2-1 Sensory Reset

When you feel a panic surge because he is silent, use this grounding tool. It breaks the cycle of hyper-vigilance.

1. **Identify 5 things you see.** (e.g., a chair, a lamp, a tree).
2. **Identify 4 things you can touch.** (e.g., the texture of your jeans, the cold desk).
3. **Identify 3 things you hear.** (e.g., traffic, a clock, your breath).
4. **Identify 2 things you smell.** (e.g., coffee, old books).
5. **Identify 1 thing you taste.** (e.g., mint, water).

The Result: How does your heart rate feel now compared to five minutes ago? This drill engages your prefrontal cortex. It pulls you out of the "alarm" brain.

Chapter 10: Heal Your Mind

Chapter 10 looked at the chemical withdrawal of a breakup. These drills help you manage the dopamine crash and cortisol spikes. You will learn to use neuroplasticity to form new, autonomous paths.

Exercise 10.1: The Withdrawal Timeline Map

Your brain is detoxing from a chemical high. Knowing the stages helps you stop blaming yourself. 2025 findings show specific timelines for this process.

1. **Identify your current day post-loss.** (e.g., Day 5).
2. **The 14-Day Goal:** For the first two weeks, your dopamine is crashing. You will feel restless and desperate. List three "dopamine replacements" for this phase. (e.g., morning sunlight, a five-minute walk, a call with a sister).
3. **The Cortisol Window:** Between weeks 3 and 6, your stress hormones will spike. You might feel "brain fog." Write a letter to your future self for this phase. Remind her that the "fog" is a biological reset. It is not a sign that you should go back.
4. **The Clarity Phase:** Weeks 6-12 are when logic returns. What are three goals you want to achieve once your brain is "online" again?

Exercise 10.2: Breaking the RPE Loop

Reward Prediction Error (RPE) is the difference between what you expect and what you get. This is why social media "stalking" is so addictive.

1. **List your digital triggers.** (e.g., checking his "active" status).
2. **The Surprise Check:** Think about the last time you checked his page and felt a "high." What did you see?
3. **The Update:** Remind yourself that your brain updated its baseline. That "hit" will not be enough next time. Write this: "I am seeking a chemical spike, not a connection. This fix keeps me in withdrawal."
4. **The Action Plan:** For the next 48 hours, commit to Zero RPE. Do not look. Do not check. Write down how the "withdrawal symptoms" feel in your body.

Exercise 10.3: Memory Mismatch Protocol

Memory reconsolidation allows you to change the emotional charge of a memory. Use this three-step drill to weaken his hold. 2025 research shows this is effective for fear and attachment.

1. **Reactivation:** Briefly recall a painful memory of him being inconsistent. (Stay in it for only one minute).
2. **The Mismatch:** Immediately engage in a completely different, positive activity. For example, listen to a song he hated or go to a place he never wanted to visit with a friend.

3. **The Result:** The brain tries to restabilize the old memory but finds the new, safe association. Repeat this three times this week with the same memory.
4. **The Journal Prompt:** How has the "intensity" of that memory changed on a scale of 1-10?

Exercise 10.4: The DMN Narrative Audit

The Default Mode Network (DMN) builds stories about who you are. After a breakup, it often creates "nostalgia" or "fantasy" narratives.

1. **The Nostalgia Trap:** Write down one "perfect" memory you keep replaying.
2. **The Reality Check:** Write down the fact-based reality of that day. Was he late? Did you fight later?
3. **The Fantasy Trap:** Write down what you "hoped" he would become.
4. **The Current Fact:** Write down who he actually is today. (e.g., "He is a man who does not text me back").

Chapter 11: Quiet the Panic

Chapter 11 looked at your breath as a remote control for your nervous system. These drills use Triangle Therapy (TTB) and polyvagal tools to create internal safety.

Exercise 11.1: The Vagus Nerve Anchor

A long exhale activates the "vagus brake." It tells your brain the emergency is over.

1. **Identify a trigger.** (e.g., his name on your screen).
2. **The 4-7-8 Breath:** Inhale through your nose for 4 counts. Hold for 7 counts. Exhale slowly through your mouth for 8 counts.
3. **The Voo Toning:** On your next exhale, make a low, long "voooooo" sound. Feel the vibration in your belly.
4. **Repeat 5 times.** Does the "wired" feeling in your limbs decrease? This is a sign your parasympathetic system is coming back online.

Exercise 11.2: The Silence Exposure Challenge

Silence often triggers "annihilation panic" in women who were neglected. You feel like you stop existing when he is quiet.

1. **The 5-Minute Module:** Sit in a room with no phone and no music.
2. **Observe the panic.** If your heart races, do not run. Use your breath to stay in the chair.
3. **The Internal Dialogue:** Say out loud: "I am here. I exist in this silence. I am safe without a response."
4. **Build up.** Add 5 minutes every day until you can sit for 20 minutes in peace. This teaches your body that a "partner's pause" is survivable.

Exercise 11.3: The Cold Water "Dive Reflex"

If you are in a state of "flooding," you cannot think your way out. You need a physical reset.

1. **Go to a sink.** Fill your hands with ice-cold water.
2. **Splash your face for 10 seconds.** Ensure the water touches the area around your eyes.
3. **The Result:** Your heart rate will drop rapidly. This is a biological override for the fight-or-flight response. Use this before you send a desperate text or reply to a crumb.

Exercise 11.4: The Butterfly Hug for Containment

This drill soothes the amygdala and provides a sense of internal support.

1. **Cross your arms over your chest.** Rest your hands on your opposite shoulders.
2. **Tap in a rhythm.** Left, right, left, right.
3. **Close your eyes.** Imagine yourself as a whole, solid person. Feel the support of your own touch.
4. **The Reflection:** How does this change your urge to seek his touch for validation? You are providing the containment your nervous system needs.

Chapter 12: Unplug and Reset

Chapter 12 looked at how digital tools hijack your dopamine circuits. These drills help you restore your D2 receptors and reclaim your agency.

Exercise 12.1: The Reward Circuit Audit

We often use our phones to manage a "chemical hunger."

1. **The Mood Log:** For two days, write down how you feel *before* you open his social media. Are you bored? Anxious? Lonely?
2. **The Match Check:** Write down how you feel *after* you scroll. Do you feel better? Or do you feel more empty?
3. **The Anhedonia Test:** On a scale of 1-10, how much joy do you get from "analog" things? (e.g., a physical book, a sunset). If your score is low, your receptors are likely downregulated.

Exercise 12.2: The 72-Hour Reset Plan

A short break can change how dopamine acts in your brain.

1. **Pick a 72-hour window.** (e.g., Friday night to Monday morning).
2. **The Replacement List:** What will you do with the three hours you save? List three tasks. (e.g., painting, a walk, cooking).
3. **The Detox Log:** Write down your feelings on Day 2. Expect restlessness. This is a sign that your brain is repairing its signaling paths.
4. **The Focus Check:** On Day 4, try reading a physical book for 30 minutes. Is it easier to focus than it was on Day 1?

Exercise 12.3: The "Greyscale" and Notification Purge

Use these strategies to protect your reward system from being hijacked.

1. **Turn your phone to greyscale.** Does the screen feel less alluring now?
2. **The "Nuclear" Purge:** Turn off all notifications except for real humans in your immediate family.
3. **The Reflection:** How many times did you reach for your phone today only to realize there was no "ping" to chase? This is the restoration of your choice.

Exercise 12.4: Finding Your "Flow" State

Flow states suppress the hyper-active Default Mode Network (DMN) and enhance stability.

1. **Identify one activity that makes you lose track of time.** (e.g., gardening, puzzles, writing).
2. **The Challenge Check:** Is this task hard enough to need focus, but easy enough to finish?
3. **The Mastery Goal:** Schedule 30 minutes for this task today. Sit for 5 minutes after finishing and feel the "analog" satisfaction. Do not post it online. Let the win be yours alone.

Synthesizing the Biology of the Bond: A Deep Dive Journaling Prompt

You have now looked at the physical, chemical, and neural ways your body has been captured by an unavailable man. True healing requires you to move from the "Option Era" to the "Priority Era." Answer these questions with radical honesty.

1. **What part of your body has been the most "vocal" during this relationship?** (e.g., your stomach, your sleep, your heart). What is that part of you trying to say about your safety?
2. **Where in your life have you allowed "intermittent rewards" to replace "consistent value"?** Why do you think you became addicted to the "maybe"?
3. **If you could offer your "withdrawing brain" one promise today, what would it be?** (e.g., "I will not look at his page today," or "I will use my breath when I feel panic").
4. **Who are you becoming as your D2 receptors restore?** Describe the version of you who finds a sunset more rewarding than a late-night text from an inconsistent man.
5. **Which "analog" relationship in your life needs your attention right now?** (e.g., a parent, a friend, a pet). Reach out to them today.

The "Let Them" Theory Application

Mel Robbins suggests using two words to reclaim your power: "Let Them."

- **If he wants to leave you on "read":** Let him.
- **If he wants to choose other people over you:** Let him.
- **If he wants to be inconsistent:** Let him.

The Action: Pick one behavior of his that you have been trying to "fix." For the next seven days, say "Let him" every time he does it. Focus 100% of that redirected energy on your own reward reset. Write down how it feels to stop managing a man who does not want to be managed.

PART FOUR

THE LANGUAGE OF LIMITS

CHAPTER 13

SET LIMITS THAT PROTECT YOUR PEACE

You feel like a rubber band stretched to the point of snapping. You check your phone while you cook dinner. You reply to his vague texts while you are at work. You say "yes" to a late-night invite even when your eyes are heavy with sleep. You feel a constant, low-level buzz of anxiety in your chest. This is the sound of your peace being stolen. You have allowed your lines to blur. You have become a person who reacts to his needs while ignoring your own.

Setting limits is not about being mean or cold. It is a biological requirement for your health. When you have no limits, your body stays in a state of high alert. This chapter looks at the science of why you struggle to say "no." We look at the facts of how limits protect your brain and your body. You will learn to identify where your peace is leaking. You will find the tools to set firm, kind limits that demand respect. You stop being an option when you decide where you end and he begins.

The Biology of the "Yes"

Why is it so hard to say "no"?. The answer starts in your brain. When someone asks you for something, your amygdala scans for threat. This is the part of the brain that manages emotions. If you fear conflict or rejection, your amygdala sounds the alarm. It sends signals that make you want to appease the other person. This is often called the "fawn" response.

Your heart rate rises. Your breath becomes short. You feel a sense of pressure to comply. You say "yes" because your nervous system thinks it is the safest choice. This is not a lack of willpower. it is an ancient survival mechanism. Our ancestors needed to stay in the group to survive. Rejection was a death sentence. Today, your brain treats a disagreement with him like a threat to your life.

When you override your own needs to keep the peace, you pay a physical price. Research from 2025 shows that chronic boundary violations trigger a constant stress response. Your cortisol levels stay high. This causes inflammation in your body. It leads to poor sleep, weight gain, and even cardiovascular issues. Each time you say "yes" when you mean "no," you are training your brain to see self-sacrifice as safety. To heal, you must teach your body that you are safe even when you set a limit.

Resentment as a Biological Signal

How do you know when you need a limit?. Listen to your feelings. Resentment is your internal compass. It is a sign that a value has been stepped on. It is the "check engine" light of your emotional health. When you feel a surge of anger after doing a favor, that is data. It tells you that you have given more than you have to spare.

Resentment often grows in the "service zone." This is a dynamic where you do the emotional work for both people. You plan the dates. You manage his moods. You fix his problems. You think that if you do enough, he will finally choose you. However, 2026 research shows that this over-functioning actually lowers your relational value. It teaches him that he does not have to put in effort because you will always bridge the gap.

To reclaim your peace, you must audit your drain. Jot down moments where you feel tired or small. Ask yourself, "What value felt ignored here?". Was it your privacy, your time, or your independence? Once you name the violation, you can start to draw the line. Limits are the tools that turn resentment into trust.

Categorizing Your Peace

Limits come in many forms. You must be specific about what you are protecting. Recent clinical findings identify four key areas where women in the "option" cycle lose their peace.

1. Time and Digital Limits

In our current world, digital access is constant. He can reach you at any hour. This blurs the line between presence and availability. You might feel a sting when you see a "seen" receipt with no reply. This anxiety drains your focus.

Set rules for your devices. Decide when you will be offline. For example, tell yourself: "I do not check texts after 9 p.m." or "I do not reply to vague 'hey' messages." This protects your "One Time", the time you spend alone to recharge. It signals that your time is a limited and valuable resource.

2. Emotional Limits

You have the right to share your history at your own pace. You do not have to "trauma-dump" on the first date to be real. Emotional limits protect your feelings and your past. They prevent "emotional flooding," where you share too much too soon without trust. A healthy partner will respect a phrase like, "I'm not ready to talk about that yet."

3. Financial and Resource Limits

Couples who talk about money early experience less stress. Set rules for spending and lending. If a man asks to borrow money in the first few dates, that is a red flag. Protecting your financial peace is an act of self-respect. It ensures you are not entering a relationship from a place of scarcity.

4. Physical Limits

Consent must be mutual and ongoing. This includes your personal space and your home. If surprise visits make you feel uneasy, state that limit. You decide who enters your space and when. A partner who values you will honor these lines without a fight.

The "Clarity Sandwich" Technique

Communicating a limit can feel nerve-wracking. To stay calm, use a research-backed method called the "Clarity Sandwich." This structure helps your brain process the limit as an opportunity rather than a threat.

1. **The Bread (Appreciation):** Start with a positive statement. "I really enjoy our time together."
2. **The Filling (The Limit):** State your requirement clearly. "I need at least two days' notice for plans."
3. **The Bread (The Benefit):** End with how this helps the connection. "This helps me be more present and excited when we meet."

This method keeps you "on your side of the net." You speak about your needs, not his flaws. It reduces defensiveness in the other person. It also engages your prefrontal cortex, the part of the brain that handles wise decision-making. You move from reacting in a panic to acting from a place of confidence.

Using the FAST Skill for Self-Respect

When you are an option, you often sell out your values to keep a man interested. The FAST tool from Dialectical Behavior Therapy (DBT) helps you stay true to yourself during hard talks.

- **Fair:** Be fair to your needs as well as his. Validate your own feelings first.
- **Apologies (None):** Stop saying "sorry" for having a standard. Do not apologize for being alive or having a preference.
- **Stick to Values:** Do not compromise your integrity to avoid a breakup. Your values are valid and non-negotiable.
- **Truthful:** Stop making up excuses for his poor behavior. Be honest about the reality of the connection.

Studies show that people who use the FAST skill regularly report 60% higher relationship satisfaction. They feel more empowered and less like victims of their environment. By being consistent, you teach others that your limits are your identity, not just suggestions.

Handling Pushback and Testing

Expect some resistance. People who benefited from your lack of limits will often test the new lines. They might call you "unreasonable" or "intense." They might use guilt to make you back down. This is a normal part of the process. it is data about the health of the connection.

Use the "Broken-Record" technique. Calmly repeat your limit in the same words. "I understand you're frustrated, but I need us to decide on plans by 5 p.m." Do not get pulled into a long debate. You do not owe anyone an explanation for your peace.

If the conversation becomes heated, take a five-minute timeout. This prevents you from saying something you will regret. It also stops the "pursuer-withdrawer" loop that traps many couples. A partner who continues to violate your clearly stated lines is showing you his priorities. Believe his actions over his words.

Reclaiming Your Energy with "Let Them"

Mel Robbins introduces a tool called the "Let Them" theory. This is a mindset shift that frees you from the burden of managing others. If he wants to be inconsistent, let him. If he wants to ignore your text for three days, let him.

When you say "let them," you stop wasting energy on things you cannot control. You detach from the outcome. You move from an external locus of control to an internal one. You focus on your own response. You ask, "What is best for my peace right now?".

This is not about giving up. it is about setting yourself free from the exhausting cycle of trying to "fix" a man who does not want to be found. It allows you to see the situation with total clarity. When you stop being the one to "save" the connection, you finally see if there is a real bond underneath the noise.

The Compounding Benefit of Peace

Setting limits is a skill that gets stronger with use. Each time you stand up for your needs, you strengthen the neural pathways associated with confidence. You are literally rewiring your brain for resilience.

In the 2026 dating world, emotional maturity is the most valuable asset. Partners who respect themselves attract partners who do the same. Boundaries do not push the right people away; they invite them in. They create the conditions where a real priority can flourish.

Your peace is your most precious resource. It is the foundation for your mental and physical health. Do not let it be an afterthought. Make it your first goal. You stop being an option the moment you realize that your peace is worth more than his approval. Choose your limits. Choose your peace. Choose yourself today.

Scientific Note on Neuroception and Stress The Neuroception of Psychological Safety Scale (NPSS) measures how your nervous system perceives your environment. High scores in "body sensations" correlate with better emotional regulation. Chronic stress from an unstable partner lowers these scores. It makes you more reactive and fragile. Setting limits helps restore your neuroception of safety. It allows your system to move from a state of "defense" to one of "restoration."

CHAPTER 14

STATE YOUR NEEDS WITH CLARITY AND CONFIDENCE

You know that feeling in the back of your throat. It's a physical presence, a dry, jagged lump that sits there every time he says something "vague-adjacent." It's there when he mentions he "might" be free this weekend, or when he sends a meme at 11:00 PM after ignoring your text for three days. You want to speak. You want to ask, *"What are we doing?"* or *"Why am I the only one making effort?"*, but you swallow it. You've become an expert at swallowing the truth.

For years, we've been sold a lie: that the most attractive thing a woman can be is "low-maintenance." We've been told that if we just don't make waves, if we remain the "Cool Girl" who doesn't need labels, plans, or basic human consistency, he will eventually realize how easy life is with us and choose us.

"Low-maintenance" in the context of a one-sided relationship is just another word for "invisible." When you stop stating your needs, you don't become more attractive; you become a ghost in your own life. You are training him to treat you like a convenience because you have effectively deleted your own requirements for the sake of his comfort. This is the "Option Cycle" at its most lethal, the moment you decide that his potential presence is worth more than your actual peace.

The Neurobiology of the "Unvoiced" Pain

Why is it so hard to just say, *"I need more than this"*? It isn't because you're weak. It's because your brain is currently a victim of its own evolution.

When you feel a need, say, a need for reassurance or a scheduled date, your brain's **amygdala** (the fear center) immediately scans the situation. If you've spent months or years as an "option," your brain has likely been conditioned to associate "stating a need" with "potential abandonment." To your prehistoric brain, abandonment equals death. So, the **Dorsal Anterior Cingulate Cortex (dACC)**, the part of your brain that processes both physical pain and social rejection, lights up like a Christmas tree.

When you stay silent, you aren't being "chill." You are in a state of **Active Suppression**.

Scientifically, this causes a massive spike in **cortisol** (the stress hormone). Because you aren't expressing the need, that energy has nowhere to go. It stays in the body. This is why women in "situationships" often report chronic neck pain, digestive issues, and "brain fog." You are literally making yourself sick to avoid an uncomfortable conversation. You are setting yourself on fire to keep him warm. In this chapter, we are going to put out the fire.

The 2026 Dating Landscape: Why "Ask Culture" is Your Only Way Out

As we navigate the mid-2020s, the "vague-dating" epidemic has reached a fever pitch. With the rise of "deliberate breadcrumbing" and "soft-launching" lives that don't include a partner, the only way to survive is to adopt **Ask Culture**.

In "Guess Culture," we wait for signs. we read into the timing of a text or the choice of an emoji. We try to *guess* if he likes us enough to be serious. This is a losing game. It keeps you in a submissive, reactive state.

Ask Culture is the hallmark of the Priority Woman. She doesn't guess; she generates data. She understands that a "No" is just as valuable as a "Yes" because both provide clarity. If you ask for a commitment and he says he's "not sure," he has given you a gift. He has told you that he is not a candidate for the role you are hiring for. You haven't lost a partner; you've gained your time back.

The N.A.N. Framework: Reclaiming Your Signal

Before you can speak with authority, you have to stop the internal gaslighting. Most of us have spent so long being an "option" that we don't even know what we need anymore. We just know we feel "bad."

Use the **N.A.N. Framework** to audit your internal state:

1. **N - Notice the Sensation:** Stop looking at your phone and look at your body. Where is the discomfort? Is it a fluttering in your chest (anxiety/lack of safety)? Is it a heaviness in your stomach (dread/dishonesty)?
2. **A - Affirm the Right:** Say it out loud: *"I have the right to want a plan for Friday night."* or *"I have the right to know if he is sleeping with other people."* You have to convince yourself before you can convince him.
3. **N - Name the Need:** Strip away the fluff. Don't say, "I wish we hung out more." Say, "I need two dedicated nights a week where we aren't just watching TV."

The DEAR MAN Protocol: A Tactical Guide to Being Heard

To state a need without sounding "accusatory" (which is what he will use as an excuse to shut down), we use the **DEAR MAN** strategy from Dialectical Behavior Therapy. This isn't just "communication advice"; it's a neurological hack to keep the conversation in the **Prefrontal Cortex**, the logical brain, and out of the "fight-or-flight" limbic system.

1. D - Describe (The Objective Facts): Stick to the "Camera Lens" version of reality. If a camera was in the room, what would it see?

- *Avoid:* "You always ignore me on weekends."
- *Use:* "In the last three weeks, we haven't spoken on Saturday or Sunday until after 9:00 PM."
- *Why:* You cannot argue with facts. By starting here, you bypass his immediate urge to defend his character.

2. E - Express (The Subjective Impact): Tell him how the facts make you feel. Use "I" statements exclusively.

- *Script:* "I feel disconnected and anxious when we go days without checking in. It makes it hard for me to feel secure in our connection."
- *Note:* You are not saying he *made* you feel this way. You are sharing your internal weather report.

3. A - Assert (The Clear Requirement): This is where most women fail. They hint. They "wonder." They "wish." No. You must *Assert*.

- *Script:* "I need a consistent check-in during the day, and I need us to have our weekend plans set by Thursday evening."
- *Crucial:* Do not apologize for this. Do not say, "I'm sorry, I know you're busy." That is a "crumb-trailing" behavior.

4. R - Reinforce (The Reward for Him): Explain how meeting this need makes the relationship better for *both* of you.

- *Script:* "When I know what our plan is, I can be fully present and relaxed when I'm with you, rather than being distracted by the 'what-ifs'."

5. M - Mindful (The Broken Record): If he tries to deflect ("You're just like my ex," or "I've been so stressed at work"), do not take the bait. Stay mindful of your goal.

- *Response:* "I understand work is stressful, but I still need us to have a plan for the weekend to feel comfortable."

6. A - Appear Confident: Body language matters. No "upspeak" where your sentences sound like questions. Keep your eyes steady. If you're on the phone, keep your voice lower and slower. Speed is a sign of anxiety.

7. N - Negotiate: Be willing to meet in the middle on the *logistics*, but never on the *need*.

- *Example*: If he can't do Thursday for plans, but can do Friday morning, that's a negotiation. If he says "I just can't do plans," that is a boundary violation.

The "Let Them" Theory: The Ultimate Power Move

In 2025 and 2026, the most transformative psychological tool for women has been the **"Let Them" Theory**.

When you state a need, you are essentially opening a door. You are saying, *"Here is the path to being with me. Are you coming?"* If he says he can't meet that need, or if he calls you "too much," or if he simply disappears: **Let him.**

- If he wants to think your need for respect is "drama"- **Let him.**
- If he wants to lose a high-value woman because he's too lazy to text back - **Let him.**
- If he wants to choose his comfort over your connection - **Let him.**

The moment you try to *persuade* someone to meet your needs, you have already lost. A man who views you as a priority will see your needs as a roadmap, not a burden. He will be grateful that you told him exactly how to make you happy. A man who views you as an option will see your needs as an inconvenience. **Let him go find someone with no needs. (Hint: She doesn't exist; she's just better at lying to herself than you are.)**

The Somatic Shift: How it Feels to be "Unmuted"

The first time you use the DEAR MAN skill, your heart will likely hammer against your ribs. Your palms might sweat. This is the **Extinction Burst** of your old, "people-pleasing" self. It is the sound of a system being overhauled.

Watch what happens afterward. Whether he stays or goes, that jagged lump in your throat will disappear. The chronic tension in your shoulders will drop, because you are finally in alignment with yourself. You are no longer a "secret" even to yourself.

Exercises: Reclaiming Your Voice

- **The Scripting Exercise:** Pick one unmet need you currently have. Write out a DEAR MAN script for it. Read it out loud to a mirror. Notice where your voice falters. That is where the healing needs to happen.

- **The "No-Apology" Challenge:** For the next 48 hours, remove the words "I'm sorry" from any sentence where you are stating a preference or a need. (e.g., instead of "I'm sorry, can we go to Italian instead?" use "I'd prefer Italian tonight.")
- **The Data Collection:** State a small need to the man you're seeing. Don't make it a "heavy" talk. Just a small requirement (e.g., "I need you to pick up the phone when I call instead of texting back"). Watch his reaction. Does he lean in, or does he pull back? That is your answer.

Conclusion: The High Price of "Chill"

Being the "Cool Girl" is expensive. It costs you your mental health, your physical well-being, and years of your life that you will never get back.

Stating your needs is the filter that separates the "Wall-Builders" from the "Bridge-Builders." It is the only way to move from the "Option" category into the "Priority" category. You are not a "maybe." You are a "definitely", but only for the man who is brave enough to meet the requirements of your heart.

Stop whispering. The world, and the right man, is waiting to hear what you have to say.

CHAPTER 15

KEEP YOUR SELF-RESPECT DURING TOUGH TALKS

You've done the work of Chapter 14. You've identified your needs. You've written the script. You've even practiced it in the mirror until you almost believed yourself. Now, you are actually there. You are sitting on his couch, or you are on a FaceTime call, or you are looking across a café table, and the moment has arrived. It is time for the "Tough Talk."

Suddenly, the air feels thin. Your heart is doing a frantic tap-dance against your ribs. Your throat feels like it's been lined with sandpaper. Then, the most dangerous thing happens: the "Fawn" response kicks in.

You find yourself wanting to soften the blow. You want to add a "just" or an "I'm sorry" to the beginning of every sentence. You feel an overwhelming urge to smile, even though you're hurt, just to show him you're still "nice." You are on the verge of trading your self-respect for a moment of artificial harmony.

This chapter is about refusing that trade.

In the high-stakes dating world of 2025 and 2026, where "ghosting," "orbiting," and "situationships" are treated as the norm, keeping your self-respect during a confrontation is a revolutionary act. It is the difference between being a woman who is "handled" and a woman who is *respected*. This isn't about "winning" the argument; it's about walking away with your soul intact, regardless of whether he chooses to stay or go.

The Psychology of the "Dignity Gap"

Why do we abandon ourselves the moment things get uncomfortable? Why does a high-achieving, brilliant woman suddenly sound like she's asking for permission to exist when she talks to a man who hasn't even bothered to take her on a proper date in three weeks?

This is what I call the **Dignity Gap**. It is the space between how you *know* you should be treated and what you are willing to *tolerate* to avoid being alone.

When you enter a tough talk, your brain is often engaged in a tug-of-war between two regions:

1. **The Ventromedial Prefrontal Cortex (vmPFC):** This is the part of you that values your long-term goals and self-worth. It knows you deserve a priority partner.
2. **The Amygdala:** This is the part that smells "danger." In this case, the danger is social rejection or the loss of the "reward hit" (dopamine) you get from his attention.

If your self-respect is low, the Amygdala wins every time. You will find yourself "negotiating" your own boundaries away. You will accept his excuses ("I've just been so busy with the new startup") even when you know they are hollow. You do this because, in the moment, the pain of losing him feels greater than the pain of losing yourself.

Here is the raw truth: **The pain of losing yourself is permanent; the pain of losing him is temporary.**

The FAST Skill: Your Self-Respect Shield

In Chapter 14, we learned DEAR MAN to help us get what we want, but what if the "tough talk" doesn't go well? What if he deflects, gets angry, or starts to gaslight you? That is where we use the **FAST** skill from Dialectical Behavior Therapy (DBT). While DEAR MAN is for "Objective Effectiveness," FAST is for **Self-Respect Effectiveness**.

Let's break down the FAST acronym and how to apply it when the conversation gets "raw."

F - (Be) Fair: Be fair to HIM, but also, and most importantly, be fair to YOURSELF. Being fair to him means you don't name-call or exaggerate. Being fair to yourself means you don't minimize your own feelings.

- *Self-Betrayal:* "I know I'm probably overreacting, and I'm sure you didn't mean it..."
- *Self-Respect (FAST):* "I understand you have a lot going on, but my need for consistent communication is valid regardless of your schedule."

A - (No) Apologies: This is the hardest one for most women. We apologize for everything. We apologize for having a feeling, for asking a question, for "bringing this up," for "taking up his time." Every time you apologize for your needs, you are telling him (and your brain) that you are doing something wrong by being an adult.

- *Stop saying:* "I'm so sorry to have to talk about this again..."
- *Start saying:* "I want to discuss something that has been on my mind so we can move forward clearly."
- *The Rule:* Only apologize if you have actually done something wrong (like being late or breaking a promise). Never apologize for existing, having feelings, or setting a boundary.

S - Stick to Values: What do you believe in? If you believe that a relationship should be exclusive after three months, **stick to that**. If you believe that a man should call when he says he will, **stick to that**. When a "tough talk" happens, an avoidant or low-effort partner will often try to make your values seem "outdated," "lame," or "too much." They will try to pull you into *their* value system (where nothing matters and everything is "chill"). Don't sell out your integrity just to keep a seat at a table where you aren't being fed.

T - (Be) Truthful: Don't lie. Don't act like you're "fine" when you aren't. Don't pretend you're okay with a "casual" arrangement if you are dying for commitment. Being truthful also means being honest about the consequences. If you say, "I can't keep doing this if things don't change," you must mean it. Truthfulness is the foundation of authority.

Somatic Self-Regulation: The 2026 "Vagal Brake"

In the dating world of 2026, many "tough talks" happen via text or voice note, which is a disaster for our nervous systems. We lose the "co-regulation" of being in the same room. Our brains fill in the gaps with our worst fears.

If you are having a tough talk, you must manage your **Vagus Nerve**. The Vagus nerve is the "highway" of the parasympathetic nervous system. When it's functioning well (high vagal tone), you can stay calm even when he is being difficult. When it's "blown," you go into fight, flight, or freeze.

The 60-Second Vagal Reset (To be done *during* the talk):

1. **Exhale longer than you inhale:** This signals to the brain that there is no physical predator in the room.
2. **Feel your feet:** Literally. Press your toes into the floor. This "earthing" sensation moves the energy out of your racing heart and back into your body.
3. **The "Internal Anchor":** Imagine a literal anchor in your pelvis. No matter what he says, that anchor keeps you grounded in your truth.

When you are regulated, his words don't have the power to "topple" you. You can hear him say, "I'm just not looking for anything serious," and instead of crying or begging, you can simply say, "I appreciate the clarity. Since I am looking for something serious, it sounds like we aren't a match."

The Red Flags of a "Respect-Draining" Conversation

Not all tough talks are created equal. Some are healthy "repairs" to a relationship. Others are "traps" designed to make you feel crazy so he can avoid accountability.

You must be able to recognize when a conversation has turned from a "talk" into "emotional labor" that is costing you your self-respect. Look for these 2026-style red flags:

1. **The "Word Salad":** He talks for twenty minutes without actually saying anything. He uses corporate-speak ("I'm currently optimizing my personal growth") to avoid saying "I'm not into you."
2. **The "DARVO" Maneuver:** Deny, Attack, and Reverse Victim and Offender. You bring up a valid point (e.g., "You didn't text for four days"), and he turns it around so *you* are the one apologizing (e.g., "Well, you know I'm stressed, and your pressure is making it worse").
3. **Tone Policing:** He ignores *what* you are saying and focuses entirely on *how* you are saying it. "I would listen to you if you weren't so 'emotional'." This is a tactic to make you doubt your own voice.
4. **The "Maybe" Carrot:** He gives you just enough hope to keep you quiet. "I could see us being exclusive *eventually*, but right now ..."

If you encounter these, **stop talking.** You cannot have a productive conversation with someone who is using communication as a weapon of evasion. The most self-respecting thing you can do in this moment is to end the conversation.

The "Walk-Away" Point: The Ultimate Expression of Self-Respect

We often think that the goal of a "tough talk" is to fix the relationship. It isn't. **The goal of a tough talk is to find out if the relationship is fixable.**

There is a point in every one-sided dynamic where "talking" becomes "begging."

- If you have explained your need for consistency three times, and nothing has changed, the fourth time isn't a "talk." It's a performance of your own powerlessness.
- If you are crying and he is looking at his watch or his phone, the talk is over.

Self-respect means knowing when to stop explaining. You do not owe anyone an endless supply of "chances" to treat you with basic human decency. As we move into Part 5 of this book, we will look at how to actually walk away, but it starts here, in the middle of the talk, when you realize that your words are falling on deaf ears.

When you let go of the need to "make him understand," you regain your power. You don't need him to agree that you are a priority. You just need to *know* that you are, and act accordingly.

Scripting for Self-Respect (The FAST Method)

Let's apply FAST to a common scenario: **The "I'm Not Ready for a Label" Talk.**

The Fact: You've been seeing each other for five months. He still calls you his "friend" or "the girl I'm seeing."

Your Goal: To tell him you need exclusivity or you're leaving.

The Talk (incorporating FAST):

- **You:** "I want to talk about where we are. We've been seeing each other for five months, and I've realized that I'm not comfortable continuing without a clear commitment (Truthful/Stick to Values)."
- **Him:** "Woah, I thought we were just having fun. Why do we need to ruin it with labels? You're being so intense."
- **You (No Apologies):** "I'm not being intense; I'm being clear about what I need to feel safe in a relationship (Fair to self). I value our time together, but I value my own peace of mind more (Stick to Values)."
- **Him:** "Can't we just wait another few months and see?"
- **You (Negotiation/Truthful):** "I've already waited five months. I've realized that my 'waiting' period is over. If you aren't ready to be exclusive today, then I think it's best we stop seeing each other (The Walk-Away Point)."

Notice what you *didn't* do. You didn't say, "I'm sorry, I know I'm asking for a lot." You didn't say, "Do you think I'm pretty enough to be your girlfriend?" You stated your value, you offered him the chance to meet it, and when he declined, you accepted the "no" as data.

The Post-Talk Hangover: Protecting Your Victory

After a tough talk, especially one that ends in a breakup or a "pause," you will experience what I call the **Post-Talk Hangover.** Your dopamine will crash. Your brain will start playing a "highlight reel" of all his best moments (ignoring the four days he ghosted you). You will feel a desperate urge to text him and say, "I didn't mean it to be so heavy, I was just having a bad day."

This is the moment where self-respect is won or lost. If you cave and apologize for your boundaries, you have just taught him that your "tough talks" mean nothing. You have taught him that if he just waits a few hours, you will break yourself down for him.

Instead, do this:

1. **Block the "Rebound" Text:** Put your phone in another room.
2. **Somatic Soothing:** Take a cold shower or a long walk. Use the "Use Your Breath" techniques from Chapter 11.
3. **Write the "Why" List:** Write down every time he made you feel like an option. Read it every time you want to apologize for having standards.

Conclusion: The High Price of Self-Respect

Self-respect isn't free. The price of self-respect is often the loss of people who were only comfortable with you when you were "small."

In the dating landscape of 2026, you will be told a thousand times that being "chill" is the path to love. It is a lie. Being "chill" is the path to being an option. Being "clear" and "self-respecting" is the path to being a priority.

When you keep your self-respect during a tough talk, you are doing something much bigger than just managing a relationship. You are healing the "Part of You That Feels Unseen" (Chapter 8). You are "Trusting Your Body to Sense Danger" (Chapter 9). You are finally, after years of silence, choosing yourself.

You might lose him, but you will have *you.* and in the end, that is the only relationship that is truly non-negotiable.

CHAPTER 16

STOP DOING ALL THE EMOTIONAL HEAVY LIFTING

You are tired. It is a specific, soul-deep exhaustion that sleep cannot fix. It is the fatigue of the woman who has become the primary investigator, the lead strategist, and the sole crisis manager of a relationship that should be a partnership. For months, perhaps years, you have been the one carrying the mental load. You are the one who remembers the anniversaries, the one who initiates the "talks," the one who deciphers his moods like a coded telegram, and the one who makes the plans.

Every morning, you wake up and mentally scan the horizon for his emotional weather. If he is distant, you brainstorm ways to pull him closer. If he is stressed, you curate the perfect supportive text. If the connection feels stagnant, you are the one researching weekend getaways or "connection exercises."

Yet, you eventually realize a devastating truth: if you stopped pulling, the entire structure would collapse into the abyss.

This is emotional heavy lifting. It is the act of over-functioning to compensate for a partner's under-functioning. It is a survival strategy born of fear, the fear that if you don't do the work, the work won't get done, and the person you love will simply drift away. In this chapter, we are going to put down the ropes. We are going to explore the neurobiology of the "fixer" brain, the high cost of relational over-performance, and the transformative power of allowing a vacuum to exist.

The invisible work: defining the load

Emotional labor is often invisible, which is why it is so insidious. It is the "cognitive grease" that keeps a relationship moving. In a healthy, priority-based connection, this labor is shared. One person leans in when the other is weak; the load shifts back and forth like a well-coordinated dance.

In an "option" dynamic, the scale is permanently tilted. You have taken on the role of the Relational Architect. You are doing the following:

1. **Anticipatory Management:** You spend hours predicting his needs so he never has to experience discomfort. You handle his moods before they even happen.
2. **The Initiation Tax:** You are the only one who starts conversations that matter. If you didn't ask "How was your day?" or "How are you feeling about us?", the silence would be deafening.
3. **Digital Maintenance:** In the 2026 dating landscape, this looks like being the one who constantly "likes," comments, and keeps the digital pulse of the relationship alive while he remains a passive observer.
4. **Moral Reconciliation:** You spend time explaining *his* behavior to *yourself*. You act as his defense attorney in the court of your own mind, making excuses for his lack of effort so you don't have to face the reality of his indifference.

The weight of this work is immense. It drains your creative energy, your professional focus, and your joy. You have become so busy managing the relationship that you have forgotten how to actually *be* in it.

The neurobiology of the "fixer's" high

Why do we keep doing it? Why do we continue to pull the ropes even when our hands are bleeding? The answer lies in the dopamine-reward system of the brain.

When you "fix" a problem in the relationship, when you send that perfect text that gets him to reply, or when you plan a date that makes him smile, your brain receives a hit of dopamine. This is the "Fixer's High." For a brief moment, you feel in control. You feel like you have successfully "managed" the connection.

However, this is an addictive loop. Your brain begins to associate your labor with safety. You believe that as long as you are working, the relationship is secure. This creates a state of chronic hyper-vigilance. Your **Prefrontal Cortex** is constantly "on," scanning for potential threats to the bond.

Over time, this leads to **Adrenal Fatigue**. Your body is not designed to live in a state of perpetual relational maintenance. The constant output of cortisol and norepinephrine eventually leads to "burnout," where you feel numb, resentful, and physically depleted. You are essentially running a marathon every day for someone who won't even walk to the mailbox for you.

The "Step Back" strategy: creating the vacuum

The most terrifying thing a "fixer" can do is stop fixing. The fear is that if you stop, everything will end.

Nonetheless, this is exactly what you must do. To move from being an option to being a priority, you must create a vacuum. A vacuum is a space where his effort, or lack thereof, becomes visible.

If you are always the one pulling the ropes, he never feels the weight of the bridge. He has no incentive to work because you are doing it all for him. By stepping back, you are performing a "Relational Audit." You are allowing the truth of his investment to reveal itself.

How to implement the Step Back:

1. **Cease All Initiation:** For one week, do not be the first one to text, call, or suggest a plan. This is not a game; it is an experiment in data collection.

2. **Stop the Defense:** When he fails to show up or forgets an important detail, do not make an excuse for him. Let the disappointment sit in the room.
3. **End the Research:** Stop reading books (except this one!), listening to podcasts, or asking friends for advice on "how to get him to..." If the relationship requires a PhD to understand, it is not a relationship; it is a project.
4. **Recenter Your Energy:** Every time you feel the urge to "manage" him, redirect that energy toward a project that is entirely about *you*.

Creating this space is an act of radical self-empowerment. It is the moment you decide that your energy is a finite, precious resource that will no longer be spent on someone who treats it like a free commodity.

The 2026 "Effort Deficit" and the Rise of the Passive Partner

In the current era, technology has made it easier than ever to be a passive partner. "Soft-launching" a life together through social media tags can often mask a total lack of actual, real-world effort. Men who view you as an option have mastered the art of "Low-Calorie Connection", giving you just enough digital interaction to keep you on the hook without ever having to do the heavy lifting of true intimacy.

Passive partners rely on your willingness to over-function. They thrive on your competence. They know that if they "forget" to book the dinner, you will do it. They know that if they "don't know" how to handle a conflict, you will provide the script for them.

Stepping back breaks this cycle. It forces the passive partner to either step up or step out. If he is truly a "Wall-Builder" (as discussed in Chapter 6), your silence will be the end of the connection. While that is painful, it is also a victory. You are finally free of the weight of a dead-end bond.

The Mirroring Technique: A New Standard for Interaction

Instead of over-functioning, we are going to adopt the **Mirroring Technique**. This is a psychological tool designed to ensure that you are only investing as much as you are receiving.

Mirroring is not about being "petty" or "keeping score." It is about maintaining relational equilibrium. It is a commitment to your own dignity.

The Rules of Mirroring:

- **Match the Frequency:** If he texts once a day, you text once a day. If he takes five hours to reply, do not reply in five seconds.
- **Match the Depth:** If he shares a superficial detail about his day, do not reply with a three-paragraph essay about your deepest fears.
- **Match the Planning:** If he hasn't suggested a date in a month, do not suggest one. If the "dating" stops because you stopped planning, you have your answer.
- **Match the Vulnerability:** Only share your "raw" self with someone who is willing to be raw in return.

By mirroring his effort, you protect your heart from the "exposure" of being the only one who cares. You become a reflection of his investment. If he sees a reflection of low effort, he may choose to change his behavior, or he may simply fade away. Either way, you are no longer the one doing the heavy lifting.

Facing the void: the terror of the silence

The hardest part of stopping the heavy lifting is the silence that follows. When you stop being the architect, the house becomes very quiet. This is the moment when many women panic. They mistake the silence for "failure" and rush back to the ropes.

Please understand: The silence is not a failure. The silence is the truth.

The silence is the sound of a man who was only there because you made it easy for him to stay. The silence is the sound of a relationship that was held together by your willpower alone. Facing this void requires immense courage. You must be willing to sit in the stillness and admit that you were carrying a weight that was never yours to bear.

This is where the "inspirational" part begins. In that silence, you find your own voice again. You find the energy you had been pouring into him returning to you like a flood. You realize that you have been using your incredible strength to pull a heavy stone, when you could have been using that same strength to build a temple for yourself.

Reclaiming your creative and vital energy

Think about the sheer amount of mental space he has occupied. Think about the hours spent analyzing his texts, the nights spent crying to your friends, the days spent in a "fog" of anxiety.

What could you have done with that energy?

- Could you have started that business?
- Could you have finished that degree?
- Could you have traveled to that country you've always wanted to see?
- Could you have deepened your relationships with the people who actually show up for you?

When you stop the emotional heavy lifting, you get your life back. You move from being a "manager of a man" to being the "queen of your own domain." Every ounce of effort you withhold from an unresponsive partner is an ounce of effort you can now invest in your own brilliance.

This is the ultimate empowerment. You realize that you are not "needy", you are powerful. You were simply using your power on the wrong person. By redirecting that energy toward yourself, you become a magnet for a priority partner. A high-value man does not want a woman who will do all the work for him; he wants a woman who is so busy building her own incredible life that he has to work hard just to be a part of it.

The Scientific Shift: From Sympathetic to Parasympathetic

As you stop over-functioning, your nervous system undergoes a profound shift. You move out of the "Sympathetic" (fight-or-flight) state and back into the "Parasympathetic" (rest-and-digest) state.

Research into relational dynamics shows that women who "over-care" often have elevated levels of **Cortisol** and **Prolactin**, which can interfere with sleep and metabolic health. By stepping back and letting go of the heavy lifting, you allow your body to recalibrate. Your heart rate variability (HRV) improves. Your sleep deepens. Your "brain fog" clears.

You are literally healing your biology by refusing to do his emotional work. You are choosing your health over his convenience.

Conclusion: The Freedom of the Open Hand

There is a profound peace in the open hand. A closed, strained hand, the hand that is white-knuckled on the ropes, is a hand that cannot receive anything new.

By letting go of the heavy lifting, you are opening your hands. You are saying to the universe, "I am no longer available for one-sided labor. I am no longer interested in being an architect for someone who won't even pick up a hammer."

This chapter is your permission slip to be "lazy" in your relationship for a while. If it falls apart because you stopped holding it up, let it fall. The rubble will make excellent fertilizer for the life you are about to grow.

You are a priority. You are a prize, and you are officially off-duty from the emotional construction site.

CHAPTER 17

BREAK THE HABIT OF PLEASING EVERYONE ELSE

You are the woman who makes everything easy for everyone else while making life impossible for yourself. You pride yourself on your empathy, your flexibility, and your ability to "read the room." You are the "nice one," the "reliable one," and the one who never causes a scene. Yet, beneath the surface of this polished compliance, a quiet resentment is simmering. You have spent so many years perfecting the art of pleasing others that you have lost the ability to hear your own voice.

Pleasing people is not a personality trait; it is a survival strategy. It is a protective shield you built long ago to navigate a world that made you feel unsafe when you were "too much" or "too difficult." You learned that safety was found in being small, being helpful, and being exactly what other people needed you to be.

In the context of a relationship where you are treated as an option, people-pleasing becomes a trap. You believe that if you are just a little more accommodating, a little more patient, or a little more perfect, he will finally see your worth. You think you can earn a place as a priority through sheer force of compliance. Today, we are going to dismantle that illusion. We are going to look at why your brain defaults to "fawning," the chemical cost of self-betrayal, and the radical empowerment that comes from learning to be "the villain" in someone else's story.

The Fawn Response: Why your brain chooses safety over truth

Psychologists often talk about "Fight," "Flight," or "Freeze." There is a fourth response that is far more common in relational dynamics: "Fawn." This is a biological drive to appease an aggressor or a distant partner to avoid conflict or abandonment.

When you sense tension or distance in a relationship, your **Amygdala** sends a signal of alarm. For a people-pleaser, this alarm doesn't trigger a fight. Instead, it triggers a rush of **Oxytocin** and **Dopamine** linked to social bonding. Your brain tells you: "If I make them happy, I will be safe."

This is the "Fawn" response in action. You start to over-share, over-care, and over-adjust. You mirror his moods to keep the peace. You suppress your own needs because expressing them feels like a threat to the connection. This behavior is deeply rooted in the **Social Pain Network** of the brain. Since the brain processes social rejection in the same regions as physical pain, fawning is essentially a form of self-medication. You are trying to prevent the "sting" of rejection by being indispensable.

Understanding that this is a biological reflex, not a character flaw, is the first step toward freedom. You are not "weak" for wanting to please; your nervous system is simply trying to keep you alive in the only way it knows how.

The high cost of relational compliance

The tragedy of the people-pleaser is that by trying to be everything to everyone, she becomes nothing to herself. In an "option" dynamic, your willingness to please is what allows him to remain low-effort.

1. **The Erosion of Identity:** Every time you say "yes" when you want to say "no," you chip away at your sense of self. Eventually, you don't even know what you like, what you want, or who you are without someone else's approval.
2. **The Resentment Debt:** You are currently building a massive mountain of "unspoken asks." You do favors you don't want to do, and then you feel angry when he doesn't reciprocate. This creates a toxic cycle of martyrdom.
3. **The Loss of Respect:** Paradoxically, the more you please, the less you are respected. A partner who sees you as an option will never view you as a priority if you behave like a servant. Respect is earned through boundaries, not through endless accommodation.
4. **Biological Burnout:** Constant fawning keeps your body in a state of high **Cortisol**. You are perpetually scanning for shifts in his tone or body language. This leads to chronic fatigue, digestive issues, and a weakened immune system.

Your "niceness" is a tax you are paying to a person who isn't even invested in the property. It is time to stop the payments.

Rewiring the "Good Girl" Blueprint

Most people-pleasing habits are formed in childhood. You may have been rewarded for being "good" and punished for being "difficult." You were taught that your value was tied to your utility.

To break this habit, you must perform "Inner Child Work." You must go back to that little girl and tell her that she is allowed to have a "no." You must convince her that she is lovable even when she is inconvenient.

The Rewiring Process:

- **Identify the "Shoulds":** Start noticing how many of your daily actions are driven by the word "should." *I should text him back immediately. I should offer to help him with his project.* Replace "should" with "want." If the "want" isn't there, the action shouldn't be either.

- **Practice Small Rejections:** Start saying "no" to low-stakes things. Tell the barista you don't want the extra shot. Tell your friend you can't make the 6:00 p.m. dinner. Feel the discomfort in your body and watch it pass.
- **Validate Your Own Feelings:** Stop asking, "Is it okay for me to feel this way?". Your feelings are facts. You do not need a permit to be angry, disappointed, or hurt.

By rewiring these internal scripts, you move from a state of "Performance" to a state of "Presence." You stop acting for an audience and start living for yourself.

Reclaiming your agency in 2026

The modern world is a playground for people-pleasers. Social media encourages "Performative Empathy," where we feel pressured to like every post and comment on every update to maintain our social standing. In 2026, the digital mental load is heavier than ever.

You are likely "Digital Fawning": replying to his crumbs with excessive emojis, staying active on his stories so he knows you're "there," and curate-ing your own life to appeal to his tastes. This is a waste of your precious cognitive energy.

Reclaiming your agency means opting out of the "Like Economy." It means realizing that his "seen" receipt is not a judgment on your worth. It means having the courage to be "unfollowed" or "unliked" by anyone who does not treat you as a priority. Your digital footprint should be a reflection of your own joy, not a lure for his attention.

The radical act of disappointing others

This is the most important lesson in this chapter: You must become comfortable with disappointing people.

If you are a priority woman, you will inevitably disappoint people who want you to remain an option. You will disappoint the man who wants a "chill girl" who never asks for commitment. You will disappoint the friends who rely on your emotional labor to fix their lives.

Disappointment is the price of admission for a life of integrity. When you set a boundary, someone will get upset. That upset is not your responsibility. It is their reaction to no longer having unlimited access to your energy.

The Disappointment Mantra: *"I would rather disappoint you than betray myself."*

Repeat this every morning. Let it sink into your bones. Every time you choose your own peace over someone else's convenience, you are casting a vote for the woman you are becoming.

The "No" Workout: Building your boundary muscle

Boundaries are the guardrails of self-respect. For a people-pleaser, setting a boundary feels like an act of war. However, a boundary is actually an act of love—it tells people how they can be in a relationship with you without destroying you.

How to use the "No" Workout:

1. **The 24-Hour Rule:** When someone makes a request, never say "yes" immediately. Say, "Let me check my schedule and get back to you." This creates a "cooling off" period for your fawning reflex.
2. **The "No" Without a "But":** Stop explaining your "no." You do not need a valid excuse to protect your time. "I can't make it" is a complete sentence. Adding a "Because" gives the other person a chance to negotiate your boundaries.
3. **The Selective Silence:** You are not an emergency service. If he texts you a low-effort crumb at 11:00 p.m., you do not have to reply. Let him sit in the silence of your absence.
4. **The Priority Audit:** Once a week, look at your calendar. How many of these activities were for *you*? How many were to keep someone else happy? Shift the ratio toward yourself.

As you build this muscle, the fear of being "disliked" will fade. You will realize that the people who truly value you will respect your "no." The people who only valued your utility will fall away, and that is exactly what you want.

Conclusion: The freedom of being "The Villain"

There is a strange, wild freedom in being "The Villain" in someone's story. If being the villain means you are a woman who knows her worth, sets her limits, and refuses to be an option, then wear that cape with pride.

By breaking the habit of pleasing everyone, you are finally making room to please the most important person in your life: You. You are reclaiming the energy you spent on "maintenance" and putting it into "creation." You are no longer a responder; you are an initiator.

You stop being an option the moment you stop asking for permission to exist. You are the prize. You are the priority. Your "yes" is now a sacred gift that you only give to those who have earned it with consistency, respect, and love.

REFLECTION EXERCISES

CHAPTERS 13 TO 17

You have journeyed through the most challenging terrain of this book. Part 4 has shifted the focus from understanding his behavior to fortifying your own. You have learned to set boundaries, state needs, maintain self-respect during conflict, stop over-functioning, and dismantle the habit of people-pleasing. Now, we must move these concepts from the pages of this book into the neural pathways of your brain and the muscle memory of your body.

These reflection exercises are designed to be a deep-dive immersion. Find a space where your nervous system feels safe. Use these prompts to bridge the gap between the "Option" you used to be and the "Priority" you are becoming.

Chapter 13: Set Limits

Setting limits is often mistaken for an act of aggression. In reality, a boundary is an act of extreme self-care. It is the architectural plan for your peace.

Exercise 1: The Peace Perimeter Audit

Take a piece of paper and draw three concentric circles.

- **The Inner Circle (The Sanctuary):** List the behaviors, values, and types of communication that make you feel completely safe and valued. Who is allowed here? What are the requirements for entry?
- **The Middle Circle (The Gate):** List the behaviors that you find tolerable but that require monitoring. This is where "Options" usually live. What are the specific red flags that would push someone from this circle to the outer edge?
- **The Outer Circle (The Border):** List your non-negotiables. These are the behaviors that result in immediate withdrawal of your energy. Examples might include "disrespectful tone," "ghosting for more than 48 hours," or "refusal to define the relationship."

Exercise 2: The Somatic Boundary Sensor

Recall a time recently when someone crossed a boundary. Close your eyes and scan your body as you remember that moment.

- Where did you feel the "invasion"? Did your stomach tighten? Did your jaw clench? Did you feel a sudden heat in your chest?
- Label this sensation as your "Boundary Alarm."
- Write a letter to this alarm, thanking it for trying to protect you. Promise that from now on, you will listen to the physical signal instead of talking yourself out of it.

Exercise 3: The Selective Access List

We often give high-level access to low-effort people. Look at the man you are currently seeing (or the last one who made you feel like an option).

- How much access does he have to your "Sanctuary"?
- Does he have the "key" to your emotional state?

- Does he have "unlimited data" on your thoughts and vulnerabilities?
- Create a "Downgrade Plan." List three ways you can restrict his access until his effort matches your value. (e.g., "I will no longer share my deep career anxieties with him until he shows he can be consistent with weekend plans.")

Chapter 14: Clarity and Confidence

A need is a requirement for the relationship to function; it is not a suggestion. Moving from "Guess Culture" to "Ask Culture" requires a total overhaul of your communication style.

Exercise 4: The Internal Needs Inventory

Distinguishing between a "want" and a "need" is critical. A "want" is a preference (e.g., "I want him to like the same movies as me"). A "need" is a necessity for your nervous system to stay regulated (e.g., "I need to know when our next date is").

- List five things you are currently "hoping" he will do.
- Filter these through the "Priority Lens." Which of these are actually needs?
- Select the most pressing need and apply the **N.A.N. Framework** (Noticed, Affirmed, Needed). Write out what you have noticed about your body, how you affirm your right to this need, and the exact name of the need itself.

Exercise 5: The DEAR MAN Sandbox

Using the script templates from Chapter 14, draft a "Tough Talk" for your most urgent need.

- **D (Describe):** Write three objective facts about the current situation. Ensure there are no "you" statements or interpretations.
- **E (Express):** Write two "I" statements explaining how those facts impact your emotional state.
- **A (Assert):** Write one clear, direct sentence stating exactly what you require. Avoid words like "maybe," "just," or "possibly."
- **R (Reinforce):** Write one sentence explaining why meeting this need will make you a better, more present partner.

Exercise 6: The Silence Tolerance Test

People-pleasers often "fill the gap" when they state a need. They say what they need and then immediately start backpedaling to make him feel better.

- Practice stating your "A (Assert)" sentence out loud.
- After the sentence, count to ten in your head.
- Notice the urge to apologize. Notice the urge to say, "I know you're busy."
- Commit to "Holding the Gap." The first person to speak after a need is stated usually loses their leverage. Let him be the one to fill the silence.

Chapter 15: Maintain Your Self-Respect

Winning an argument is irrelevant if you lose your dignity in the process. The **FAST** skill is your anchor when the waters of conflict get choppy.

Exercise 7: The Dignity Gap Visualization

Think of the "Highest Version" of yourself, the woman who is already a priority. Imagine her sitting in a chair across from you.

- How does she sit? How does she breathe?
- Ask her: "What is the minimum level of respect I should accept in this conversation?"
- Write down her answer. Carry this note in your pocket the next time you have a confrontation.

Exercise 8: The FAST Checklist Autopsy

Recall your last difficult conversation with a romantic interest. Grade yourself on the FAST scale (Fair, No Apologies, Stick to Values, Truthful).

- Where did you falter?
- Did you apologize for having a feeling?
- Did you abandon your values (e.g., agreeing to be casual when you want commitment) just to end the tension?
- Re-write that entire conversation as if you had used the FAST skill perfectly. How would the outcome have changed? Even if he still left, how much better would *you* feel about yourself?

Exercise 9: The Post-Talk Somatic Reset

Conflict triggers the "Fight or Flight" system. You must have a plan to bring your body back to safety after a tough talk.

- Design your "Self-Respect Sanctuary" ritual. This might include a cold shower to reset the Vagus nerve, a specific playlist that makes you feel powerful, or a "No-Contact Window" of four hours to prevent the "Rebound Apology" text.
- Practice this ritual even when you aren't in conflict, so your body knows that "rest" always follows "expression."

Chapter 16: Stop Doing All the Emotional Heavy Lifting

The "Fixer" brain is addicted to the labor of love. Breaking this addiction requires you to step back and face the terrifying reality of his actual investment.

Exercise 10: The Heavy Lifting Ledger

For the next three days, keep a literal tally of your emotional labor versus his.

- **Your Side:** Every time you check his social media, analyze a text, initiate a conversation, suggest a plan, or manage his mood, give yourself a point.
- **His Side:** Every time he initiates, plans, asks how you are, or follows through on a commitment, give him a point.
- Look at the final score. Is this a partnership, or is it a solo construction project?

Exercise 11: The Mirroring Experiment

Commit to one week of "Perfect Mirroring."

- If he sends a one-word text, you send a one-word text.
- If he doesn't call, you don't call.
- If he asks you to "hang out" last minute, you mirror his level of planning by having "other plans" (even if those plans are just reading this book).
- Journal about the anxiety this causes. What is your brain telling you will happen if you stop over-functioning? "He'll forget about me." "He'll find someone else." Recognize these as "Scarcity Myths."

Exercise 12: The Vacuum Diary

When you stop pulling the ropes, a vacuum is created.

- Describe the silence. How does it feel in your body?
- Is the silence "empty," or is it "peaceful"?
- What information is the silence giving you about him?
- Write down three things you can do with the energy you are saving by not "managing" him. (e.g., "I will use the two hours I usually spend analyzing his silence to work on my side hustle.")

Chapter 17: Stop Pleasing Everyone Else

The "Fawn" response is the most subtle thief of self-worth. Breaking it requires you to become comfortable with being "the villain" in the eyes of those who want you to stay small.

Exercise 13: The People-Pleasing Autopsy

Identify your "Origin Story" of people-pleasing.

- Who was the first person you felt you had to "manage" or "appease" to be safe?
- What was the specific "price" you had to pay to be the "Good Girl"?
- List three ways you are currently acting like that child in your adult relationship.
- Gently tell that child version of yourself: "We are safe now. We don't have to be perfect to be loved."

Exercise 14: The "No" Workout

Commit to saying "no" to three things this week that have nothing to do with him.

- Say no to an extra task at work.
- Say no to a social invitation you don't actually want to attend.
- Say no to a family member's request for emotional labor.
- Notice the "Guilt Spike." Breathe through it. Realize that the guilt is just the sound of an old habit dying.

Exercise 15: The Villain Origin Story

Write a short story or a letter where you are the "Villain."

- In this story, you are the woman who says "No" to the crumbs.
- You are the woman who ends the "situationship" because it doesn't meet her standards.
- You are the woman who stays home and eats pasta alone instead of going to a party she's "expected" to attend.
- How does this "Villain" version of you feel? Is she actually evil, or is she just ... free?

The Part 4 Synthesis: Integrating the Language of Limits

You have explored the dark corners of your compliance and the bright potential of your boundaries. To conclude this section, we must weave these threads together.

Final Mission: The Priority Proclamation

Based on everything you have discovered in Chapters 13 to 17, write your personal "Priority Proclamation." This is a one-page document that outlines exactly how you will be treated moving forward.

Include sections on:

1. **Communication Standards:** (e.g., "I will only respond to plans made 24 hours in advance.")
2. **Emotional Reciprocity:** (e.g., "I will only invest emotional energy in those who demonstrate consistent curiosity about my life.")
3. **Self-Respect Protocols:** (e.g., "I will never apologize for my needs or my boundaries.")
4. **The Exit Clause:** (e.g., "If my peace is consistently compromised, I will choose my solitude over this connection.")

Sign and date this document. Read it every morning for the next thirty days.

Biological Reflection: The Shift in Your Nervous System

As you complete these exercises, your biology is changing. You are moving from a state of "Social Hyper-vigilance" to a state of "Autonomic Safety."

The Vagal Tone Check-In: Sit quietly and place your hand on your heart.

- How is your resting heart rate?
- How is the quality of your breath?
- Do you feel "lighter," or do you feel a "solidness" in your core?
- This is the sound of your **Vagus Nerve** recalibrating. You are no longer a "prey animal" scanning for the predator's mood. You are an "Apex Priority," grounded in your own territory.

The language of limits is not a set of rules for *him* to follow. It is a set of rules for *you* to live by. You cannot control whether he chooses to become a priority partner. However, by mastering Part 4, you have ensured that he no longer has the power to make you an option.

You have found your voice. You have drawn your lines. You have reclaimed your energy.

Now, we move to Part 5: Reclaiming the Woman Within. This is where the reconstruction truly begins. You aren't just surviving a bad dynamic anymore; you are building a life so incredible that any man who wants to be in it will have to be nothing short of extraordinary just to keep up.

PART FIVE

RECLAIMING THE WOMAN WITHIN

CHAPTER 18

FIND YOUR VOICE AFTER YEARS OF SILENCE

Silence in an "option" relationship is rarely quiet. It is a loud, vibrating pressure that sits in the back of your throat like a stone. For years, you may have learned that your words are dangerous. You discovered that expressing a need led to a "reset" in his behavior: a withdrawal, a cold shoulder, or the dreaded "you're too much" label. Over time, you began to curate your thoughts before they reached your lips. You edited your soul until it was small enough to fit into the gaps he left for you.

Reclaiming your voice is not just about talking. It is about the radical act of existing out loud. It is the moment you decide that your internal truth is more important than the temporary peace of his approval. This chapter is about the journey from the "Cool Girl" silence back to the vibrant, messy, and powerful resonance of your own identity.

The Anatomy of the Stifled Voice

We often think of silence as a choice, but in the context of a lopsided relationship, it is often a survival mechanism. Evolutionary psychologists, such as Matias (2016), suggest that humans have historically used emotional suppression to avoid social marginalization in stratified groups. In your relationship, you may have subconsciously viewed him as the "high-status" partner who held the power of commitment. To stay in his orbit, you suppressed your fear, your disappointment, and your desires.

This suppression creates a "weak-link" pattern in intimacy. Research shows that when even one partner suppresses their emotions, relationship satisfaction plummets for both parties. Your silence did not save the relationship; it simply ensured that the relationship remained shallow. You were physically present but emotionally invisible.

The Biological Price of "Playing It Cool"

Your body knows when you are lying to yourself. While you might appear calm on the outside, nodding along to his vague plans or swallowing your hurt when he forgets an important date, your internal systems are in a state of high alert. Studies using skin conductance and pulse monitors show that individuals who suppress their emotions experience a significant spike in sympathetic nervous system activity.

> **Scientific Note: The "Silent Stress" Response** Chronic suppression of the voice activates the Dorsal Vagal response. This is a "freeze" state where the body conserves energy because it feels it cannot fight or flee the emotional threat. While you may feel "numb" or "disconnected," your heart rate often increases, and your muscles remain in a state of micro-tension. This "racing heart in a still body" is the signature of a voice that has been silenced for too long.

This chronic state of "silent stress" has long-term health implications. It can lead to hypertension, digestive issues, and even a weakened immune system because the body is constantly diverting resources to manage the internal pressure of unexpressed truth. Your silence is literally making you tired.

Reclaiming the Throat: Somatic Voice Activation

Before you can speak your truth to him, you must first let your voice live in your own body again. The throat is the gateway between the heart and the head. In many somatic traditions, this is referred to as the "Vishuddha" or throat chakra, the center of authentic expression. When this center is blocked by years of being an "option," you may feel a physical tightness in your jaw or a "lump" in your throat when you try to speak up.

Exercise: The Lion's Roar (Simhasana) This practice is designed to release the muscular armor around the jaw and throat.

1. Kneel or sit comfortably with your spine tall.
2. Inhale deeply through your nose.
3. As you exhale, open your mouth wide, stick out your tongue toward your chin, and make a loud, forceful "haaaa" sound.
4. Visualize years of swallowed words and "it's fine" lies leaving your body with the breath.

Exercise: The Humming Bee (Brahmari) Vagus nerve stimulation is a powerful way to move out of the "freeze" state and back into "social engagement."

1. Place your fingers lightly over your ears or throat.
2. Inhale and, on a long exhale, create a steady, low-pitched humming sound.
3. Feel the vibration in your chest and throat. This vibration signals to your nervous system that it is safe to make sound again.

Shifting from "Option Talk" to "Priority Talk"

Finding your voice does not mean you have to become aggressive. In fact, true vocal power is rooted in the DBT (Dialectical Behavior Therapy) principle of *Interpersonal Effectiveness*. The goal is to state your needs clearly while maintaining your self-respect.

Using the FAST Framework for Self-Respect

When you are used to being an option, you often over-apologize or "soften" your truth to make it more palatable for him. The FAST skill helps you stay firm:

- **F - (be) Fair:** Be fair to yourself. Your needs are as valid as his "need" for space or lack of commitment.
- **A - (no) Apologies:** Stop saying "sorry" for having a feeling. Do not apologize for asking where the relationship is going.
- **S - Stick to Values:** Know what your non-negotiables are. If you value monogamy and consistency, do not pretend you are okay with a "casual" dynamic.
- **T - (be) Truthful:** Stop "rounding down" your pain. If he hurt you, state it plainly without exaggeration or minimization.

The Power of "I" Statements

In the "Option Cycle," we spend a lot of time analyzing *him*. We say, "You always disappear," or "You never prioritize me." This usually triggers his defensiveness. Shifting to "I" statements keeps the focus on your internal reality, the one thing he cannot argue with.

- **Instead of:** "You make me feel like I don't matter."
- **Try:** "I feel disconnected and anxious when our plans are left vague until the last minute. I need more consistency to feel secure in this connection".

The "Let Them" Theory of Communication

A major part of finding your voice is accepting that you cannot control how he responds to it. This is where Mel Robbins' *Let Them Theory* becomes your greatest shield.

- **Let them be uncomfortable.** If your truth makes him squirm, let him squirm. You are not responsible for managing his emotional reaction to your boundaries.
- **Let them disagree.** He may not like your new voice. He may prefer the version of you that stayed quiet and "easy." Let him have that preference while you continue to speak your truth.
- **Let them leave.** The ultimate test of your voice is the willingness to let the relationship end if your truth is too much for it to hold. A voice that is only allowed to exist in a whisper is not a voice; it is a cage.

Scientific Note: The Neuroplasticity of Assertiveness

Every time you speak a small truth, you are rewiring your brain. The Anterior Cingulate Cortex (ACC), the part of your brain that monitors social rejection, becomes less reactive as you build "evidence" that you can survive a difficult conversation. You are teaching your amygdala that speaking up is not a life-threatening event. Over time, the "lump" in your throat will dissolve, replaced by a steady, calm resonance that comes from knowing you have your own back.

Conclusion: The Sound of Your Own Name

Finding your voice is the first step in reclaiming the woman within. It is the end of the era where you were a supporting character in his story. When you speak, you are not just communicating with him; you are declaring to the universe, and to yourself, that you are here, you are valid, and you will no longer be ignored.

The silence is over. Your life is about to get a lot louder, and a lot more beautiful.

CHAPTER 19

MOVE AWAY FROM PEOPLE WHO DON'T SHOW UP

There is a specific kind of loneliness that only exists when you are with someone else. It is the hollow ache of sitting across from a man who is looking at his phone, or the quiet desperation of waiting for a text that never comes. You have spent months, perhaps years, convinced that if you just provided enough warmth, enough understanding, or enough "space," he would finally materialize. You believed your presence could compensate for his absence.

Moving away from people who don't show up is not an act of cruelty. It is an act of calibration. You are finally aligning your physical location with the emotional reality of the relationship. For too long, you have been standing in an empty room, calling it a home. In this chapter, we will explore the psychology of the "Passive Partner," the biological impact of inconsistent presence, and the empowering steps required to physically and emotionally withdraw from a connection that has already ended in every way but name.

To move away, you must first acknowledge the weight of the "Emotional Debt" you have been carrying. Every time you show up for a man who doesn't show up for you, you are taking out a loan from your future self. You are spending your time, your beauty, and your sanity on a high-risk investment with zero dividends.

The "Intermittent Reinforcement" Trap: Why Your Brain Stays

Why is it so hard to leave someone who isn't even there? The answer lies in the way your brain processes inconsistency. In the context of "Option" dynamics, your brain is not addicted to the person; it is addicted to the *possibility* of the person. When a partner shows up only 20% of the time, those rare moments of presence feel like a massive victory.

This is known as a **Variable Ratio Schedule**. In behavioral psychology, this is the most addictive form of reinforcement, the same mechanism that keeps people pulling the lever on a slot machine. Because you never know *when* he will show up, you stay in a state of high alert, always "on call." Your brain begins to value his rare presence more than the consistent presence of people who actually love you. Moving away requires you to break this addiction. You must stop valuing the "peak" and start looking at the "average." When you look at the average, you realize the relationship is a desert with the occasional mirage.

Furthermore, this intermittent presence creates a "Reward Conflict" in the brain. The **Nucleus Accumbens** (the reward center) is constantly battling the **Prefrontal Cortex** (the logic center). Your logic knows he isn't showing up, but your reward center is still chasing the high of that one time he brought you flowers or called you "baby" three weeks ago. To move away, you must starve the reward center of its occasional hit.

Identifying the "No-Show" Archetypes in the 2026 Landscape

Absence isn't always physical. A man can be sitting on your couch and still be a "No-Show." In the modern dating era, where technology allows for "presence without proximity," these archetypes have become more specialized:

1. **The Digital Ghost:** He is active on social media, liking your photos and viewing your stories within minutes, but he never initiates a real conversation or suggests a fixed date. He is "showing up" for your highlight reel, but not for your life. This is a form of "relational voyeurism." He wants the view without the responsibility of the maintenance.
2. **The Crisis-Only Partner:** He disappears when things are good but "shows up" the moment he needs emotional support, a "fix," or a place to land. He uses your empathy as a charging station. Once his internal battery is at 100%, he unplugs and leaves.
3. **The Vague Planner (The "Maybe" Man):** He says "we should do something soon" or "I'll let you know about Friday," but never follows through with a time or location. He keeps you in a state of perpetual "maybe," effectively "benching" you while he explores other options.
4. **The Emotional Wall:** He is physically present for dates, he pays for dinner, and he might even be affectionate. However, he never shares his inner world. You know his favorite movies, but you don't know his fears, his dreams, or his intentions with you. He is a spectator in the relationship, not a participant.

To move away, you must stop treating these archetypes as "projects" to be fixed and start seeing them as "traps" to be avoided.

The Biological Toll of the "Waiting Room"

Living in a state of waiting is physically destructive. When you are waiting for someone to show up, your **Amygdala** is perpetually scanning for a "signal" (a text, a call, a knock). This keeps your **Sympathetic Nervous System**, the fight-or-flight branch, engaged.

Research into **Relational Uncertainty** shows that inconsistent presence causes a spike in **Cortisol** that is actually higher than the stress caused by a clean break. The "not knowing" is what kills your peace. Over time, this chronic stress leads to:

- **Cognitive Tunneling:** Your field of vision narrows. You become so focused on his absence that you lose focus on your career, your hobbies, and your health.

- **Emotional Dysregulation:** Your "resilience tank" is empty. You find yourself crying over a dropped spoon or snapping at a coworker because you have been holding your breath for a text for three days.
- **The Suppression of Oxytocin:** Because you don't feel "safe" in the connection, your body stops producing the bonding hormone that facilitates rest and repair. You are essentially "bonding" to the stress, not the person.

Moving away is not just a lifestyle choice; it is a medical necessity. You are moving your body out of a "Waiting Room" and back into a "Living Room."

The "Withdrawal" Strategy: How to Physically and Mentally Move Away

Moving away is a process of **Decoupling**. You are untangling your nervous system from his. This requires a transition from "Hope-Based Planning" to "Fact-Based Action."

1. The "Contact Diet" and the 72-Hour Rule Stop being the one who initiates. If he doesn't show up in your inbox, do not go looking for him. This is not about "playing games"; it is about protecting your energy. Implement the 72-hour rule: if he disappears for three days without a valid reason, you treat the relationship as "inactive." If the conversation dies because you stopped providing the CPR of constant initiation, let it stay dead.

2. The Physical Distance Rule: Stop Reserving the Space If he is a "No-Show" for plans, stop inviting him. Stop leaving an empty chair at your table. Start filling your life with events and people that have a 100% "Show Up" rate. If you want to see a movie, ask a friend who you *know* will be there at 7:00 PM. By filling your physical schedule with reliable people, you make his absence irrelevant.

3. The Social Media "Mute" and the Dopamine Reset Seeing his face or his "Active Now" status triggers a dopamine spike that resets your withdrawal clock. It keeps you tethered to the "possibility" of him. Mute his stories and posts. You need a "Clean Room" for your brain to heal. In 2026, out of sight truly is the beginning of out of mind.

4. The "No-Explanation" Exit You do not owe a long, emotional speech to someone who hasn't been present. A man who isn't showing up won't "hear" your explanation anyway, he will only see it as more emotional labor he can consume. Moving away is a quiet act. It is a slow, dignified fade into your own brilliant life.

Facing the Void: Reclaiming the Empty Space

The hardest part of moving away is facing the empty space he left behind. For a long time, that space was filled with your *longing* for him. You were so busy wondering "where is he?" that you forgot to ask "where am I?". Now that you've stopped waiting, the space is just... empty.

However, emptiness is the precursor to creation. In the vacuum of his absence, you will find a wealth of resources you forgot you had:

- **Time Recovery:** You suddenly have 10-15 hours a week back that you used to spend waiting, worrying, and analyzing screenshots with your friends.
- **Mental Clarity:** Without the "Static" of his inconsistency, you can finally hear your own intuition again. Your inner voice, which has been screaming "this isn't enough," will finally be loud enough to follow.
- **Vital Force:** You will be shocked at how much energy returns to your body once you stop pouring it into a black hole. Your skin will look better, your sleep will deepen, and your creativity will spark.

The Philosophy of the "Open Hand"

To move away, you must adopt the philosophy of the open hand. A closed, clenching hand is trying to trap something that doesn't want to stay. An open hand allows the "No-Show" partner to drift away, but it also leaves the hand free to receive something new.

When you move away from people who don't show up, you are signaling to the universe that you are no longer available for "Partial Presence." You are raising the price of admission to your life. You are deciding that you would rather be alone and grounded than "with someone" and anxious.

Healing the "Absentee" Wound

Often, we stay with people who don't show up because they mirror someone from our past who also didn't show up. If you had a parent who was physically present but emotionally distant, your nervous system might mistake "absence" for "safety" or "familiarity."

Moving away from a "No-Show" partner is an act of reparenting. You are telling that younger version of yourself: "I see you waiting. I see how much it hurts to be ignored. I am taking us out of this house. We are going somewhere where we are seen." This is how you break the generational cycle of being an option.

Conclusion: The Dignity of the Departure

There is a profound dignity in walking away from a table where love is no longer being served. It is not an act of anger; it is an act of self-honor. By moving away from people who don't show up, you are making a powerful statement to yourself: *"My presence is a prize, and I will no longer waste it on an audience of one who isn't even in his seat."*

You are moving toward yourself. You are moving toward the people who hear your voice the first time you speak. You are moving toward a life where "showing up" is the bare minimum requirement for entry. You are no longer the woman who waits; you are the woman who leads.

CHAPTER 20

LEAN ON YOUR REAL SUPPORT SYSTEM

The "Option Cycle" is a masterclass in isolation. When you are pouring your vital energy into a man who treats you like a secondary character, you often find yourself pulling away from the people who treat you like the lead. You stop going to brunch with your best friends because you're waiting for a text that might arrive at noon. You stop calling your sister because you're exhausted from analyzing a three-word message for the fourth hour in a row. You feel a strange sense of shame, a "relational embarrassment," that keeps you from being honest about how little you are actually receiving.

Reclaiming the woman within requires a radical reorientation. You must stop trying to get water from a dry well and turn back toward the lush, flowing springs of your genuine support system. This chapter is about identifying who your "Real Ones" are, understanding the neurobiology of safe social connection, and learning how to leverage your community to break the addiction to an inconsistent partner.

The Architecture of the True Support System

Not every friend is a support system. In the context of healing from an "option" dynamic, you need more than just a "wingwoman" or a "venting partner." You need a structured network of people who provide different types of support. To move from being an option to being a priority, you must surround yourself with people who already view you as one.

1. The Emotional Anchor

This is the person who allows you to be "messy." They don't judge you when you admit you checked his Instagram for the tenth time today. They listen without immediately trying to fix you, providing what psychologists call **Validation-First Support**. Their presence lowers your cortisol simply by existing in your space.

2. The Truth-Teller

This friend is your "Reality Check." While the Anchor provides comfort, the Truth-Teller provides the mirror. They are the ones who say, "He hasn't called you in three days, and you deserve better than that." They help you fight the **Cognitive Dissonance** that keeps you stuck in the cycle of making excuses for him.

3. The Distraction Architect

Healing isn't all about processing; sometimes it's about *not* processing. This friend is the one who drags you to a pottery class, a hike, or a movie where phones are strictly prohibited. They help you engage your **Dopamine-Reward System** through activities that have nothing to do with romance.

4. The Mentor

This is someone who has been where you are and has successfully moved into a "Priority" life. They provide the **Neural Blueprint** for what is possible. Watching them thrive without the validation of a "low-effort" man teaches your brain that safety and joy are available elsewhere.

The Science of "Co-Regulation"

Why can't we just heal alone? The answer is biological. Humans are "obligate gregarious" creatures. Our nervous systems are not closed loops; they are open systems that co-regulate with those around us.

When you spend time with a safe friend, your **Vagus Nerve** receives "safety signals" from their facial expressions and tone of voice. This triggers the release of **Oxytocin**, the "bonding hormone", which acts as a direct antagonist to **Cortisol**. Oxytocin doesn't just make you feel good; it actually repairs the damage caused by chronic stress. It strengthens your immune system and improves your Heart Rate Variability (HRV).

Spending three hours with a man who makes you feel like an option keeps you in a state of "threat." Spending three hours with a support system that makes you feel like a priority moves you into a state of "safety." You cannot think your way out of a trauma bond; you must *relate* your way out of it. By leaning on others, you are literally using their regulated nervous systems to help settle yours.

Overcoming the "Shame Barrier"

The biggest obstacle to leaning on your support system is the belief that you are a "burden" or that you are "pathetic" for still caring about someone who doesn't care about you. This shame is a byproduct of the **Fawn Response**. You have been conditioned to believe that your value is based on how little you need from others. You want to appear "chill" and "independent."

However, true independence is actually built on a foundation of **Secure Dependency**. When you know you have a safety net, you are more likely to take the risk of walking away from a bad situation.

Exercise: The Shame Audit

1. Write down the one thing about your current relationship dynamic that you are most afraid to tell your friends.
2. Ask yourself: "If my best friend told me this exact same thing, would I judge her or would I want to hold her hand?"
3. Realize that by hiding your struggle, you are denying your friends the opportunity to love the *real* you, not just the "Cool Girl" mask you wear.

The "Village" Strategy: Diversifying Your Emotional Portfolio

Investors know that you never put all your money into one volatile stock. Yet, when we are in an "option" relationship, we put 90% of our emotional "capital" into one person who provides zero return on investment.

Reclaiming your life means **Diversifying your Emotional Portfolio**:

1. **The 30/70 Rule:** For every hour you spend thinking about or interacting with the "Option" partner, you must spend at least two hours engaging with your real support system.
2. **The "Check-In" Ritual:** Once a week, have a scheduled call or coffee with someone who has *no* connection to your dating life. Talk about books, politics, or your career. Remind your brain that you are a multifaceted human being.
3. **The Communal Ask:** Practice asking for small things. "Can you help me pick out a new plant?" "Can I call you for ten minutes while I walk to my car?" This builds the "muscle" of receiving, which has likely atrophied during your time with a low-effort partner.

Moving from "Trauma Bonding" to "Tandem Healing"

Sometimes, your support system will include others who are also healing. While this can be powerful, beware of **Co-Rumination**, the act of obsessively talking about the "Option" partner without moving toward a solution. To turn a vent session into a healing session, use a structured approach:

- **Identify the Feeling:** "I feel small when he ignores my texts."
- **Identify the Need:** "I need to feel like I'm moving toward someone who sees me."
- **Identify the Action Step:** "Tonight, let's talk about our travel plans for next summer instead of talking about him."

The Biology of Belonging: Rebuilding the Social Brain

When you have been an option for too long, your **Prefrontal Cortex** (PFC), the part of the brain responsible for long-term planning and logic, becomes "offline" due to the constant stress of the bond. Your support system acts as an "External PFC." They can see the logic that you are currently too clouded to see.

By leaning on them, you are literally using their brain power to help regulate yours. As you spend more time in "Priority" circles, your **Anterior Cingulate Cortex** (the area that monitors social standing) starts to receive new data. It realizes: "I am high-status here. I am loved here. I am a priority here." This resets your baseline for what is acceptable in a relationship.

Conclusion: You Were Never Meant to Carry This Alone

The greatest lie the "Option Cycle" tells you is that you are alone in your struggle. It makes you feel like a solitary failure. But when you lean on your real support system, you realize that your strength doesn't come from your ability to endure neglect; it comes from your ability to accept love.

Your friends, your family, your mentors, they are the ones who know your "Priority" self. They remember the woman you were before you started editing yourself for him. Let them hold the light for you until you are strong enough to carry it yourself. You are not an option. You are the center of a beautiful, vibrant village. It's time to go home.

CHAPTER 21

BUILD A LIFE THAT YOU LOVE ALONE

For a long time, the word "alone" has likely felt like a threat. In the "Option Cycle," solitude is often framed as a failure, the empty space where a text should be, the quiet Saturday night that proves he didn't choose you. You have been conditioned to view your solo time as a "waiting room" for a relationship. You weren't living; you were just paused, holding your breath until someone else's presence gave you permission to exhale.

Reclaiming the woman within requires a total rebrand of your solitude. Chapter 21 is about the shift from *Loneliness* (a state of lack) to *Solitude* (a state of abundance). It is about building a life so rich, so textured, and so deeply satisfying that a man's presence becomes a "complement" rather than a "completion." This is the final stage of becoming a Priority: creating a world that you are unwilling to shrink just to fit someone else's limited capacity.

The Psychology of "Autonomous Joy"

Most of our cultural narratives tell women that their "real life" begins when they find a partner. This creates a psychological dependency where your hobbies, your travel, and even your home decor are treated as "temporary" until a man arrives to finalize them. You might buy the "good" candles but save them for a date night that never happens. You might want to travel to Italy but hold off because "that's a romantic trip" you should save for a future boyfriend.

Psychologist Abraham Maslow identified **Self-Actualization** as the highest human need. However, you cannot self-actualize if you are perpetually "other-focused." When you are an option, your brain's **Executive Function** is hijacked by the need to monitor someone else's interest level. By deciding to build a life you love alone, you reclaim that cognitive energy for your own development. You stop being a satellite orbiting his sun and start becoming your own solar system.

Autonomous Joy is the ability to generate your own "Reward Chemicals" (Dopamine, Serotonin) without a third-party validator. It is the realization that the sunset is just as beautiful, the pasta is just as delicious, and the promotion is just as significant whether there is a man in the room to see it or not. When you master autonomous joy, you become "un-ghostable" because your happiness isn't tied to his response time.

The Biological Reset: From External to Internal Regulation

In Chapter 9, we discussed how the "Option" dynamic keeps you in a state of external regulation, you need his text to feel calm, his compliment to feel beautiful, and his presence to feel safe. Building a life alone is the ultimate "Nervous System Reset."

When you consistently choose activities that bring you peace and mastery, you strengthen your **Prefrontal Cortex (PFC)**. You move out of the "Search and Rescue" mode of the Amygdala and into a state of **Homeostasis**. You are teaching your body that *you* are the primary source of your own safety.

Scientific Note: The Power of Solo Mastery Engaging in "Mastery Activities": hobbies that require focus and skill, such as painting, coding, gardening, or weightlifting, triggers the release of **Endorphins**. Unlike the spikey, anxiety-laced Dopamine you get from a "breadcrumb" text, Endorphins provide a steady sense of well-being and resilience. You are literally "medicating" your heartbreak with your own competence. This process builds **Neural Plasticity**, allowing your brain to form new pathways that don't involve the "Reward Conflict" of an inconsistent partner.

The Four Pillars of the Priority Life

To build a life you love alone, you must invest in four specific areas of your "Solo Estate." This is not about "distracting" yourself until a man comes along; it is about building a foundation that makes a man optional.

1. The Sanctuary: Reclaiming Your Environment

Stop living in a "waiting room." If you've been holding off on buying those expensive linen sheets, investing in that high-end espresso machine, or painting the guest room because you're "waiting to see where things go," stop. Decorate for the woman you are today.

Your home should be a physical manifestation of your self-respect. It is a place where every object reflects your taste, your history, and your comfort. When your environment is a sanctuary, the prospect of letting a disruptive, low-effort man into your space becomes less appealing. You begin to value the peace of your own four walls more than the chaotic presence of an "Option" partner.

2. The Intellectual Pursuit: Reclaiming Your Mind

What did you used to love before you started spending four hours a day analyzing his mixed signals and scrolling through his "Following" list? Reclaiming your voice (Chapter 18) means reclaiming your curiosity.

Enroll in a course that has nothing to do with your career. Start a deep-dive research project on a topic that fascinates you. Read the books that have been sitting on your nightstand while you were busy checking your phone. This builds **Cognitive Reserve**, making you less susceptible to the "brain fog" of romantic rejection. An active mind is a mind that is too busy to ruminate.

3. The Physical Temple: Reclaiming Your Vessel

When we are "options," we often treat our bodies as objects to be "perfected" for his gaze. We diet to be seen; we dress to be wanted. Shift this focus to **Interoception**—how your body *feels* from the inside.

Move your body because it feels powerful to be strong, not because you want to "keep his interest." Lift weights to feel your own force. Stretch to feel your own space. Feed yourself high-quality fuel because you deserve to feel vibrant. When you view your body as a temple for your own spirit rather than a billboard for his attraction, your self-worth becomes unshakable.

4. The Solo Adventure: Reclaiming Your Agency

The "Solo Date" is the ultimate act of defiance against the Option Cycle. It is a declaration that your own company is a high-tier social event. Take yourself to the restaurant you've been wanting to try: sit at the bar, talk to the bartender, or bring a book. Travel to a new city alone. Navigate the airport, find the hotel, and choose the itinerary without checking with anyone else.

Every time you navigate the world alone and have a good time, you are signaling to your brain: *"I am enough of a person to be my own companion. I am not half of a whole; I am a whole."*

"The Let Them Theory" as a Solo Strategy

Mel Robbins' *Let Them Theory* is the guardian of your solo life. It prevents his behavior from leaking into your abundance.

- **Let them miss out:** If you are at a gallery opening you love and he is at home ignoring your texts, *let him.* His absence doesn't diminish the art; it only diminishes his experience. You are there for the art, not for the validation of him being next to you.
- **Let them be confused:** People in your life, including him, may wonder why you are "suddenly" so busy, why you are traveling alone, or why you aren't "available" for last-minute hangouts. *Let them.* You don't owe anyone an explanation for why you've decided to prioritize your own joy.
- **Let them stay where they are:** While you are climbing mountains (literal or figurative), he might stay in the same place, offering the same crumbs. *Let him.* You aren't looking back to see if he's following; you're looking forward at the view.

The 168-Hour Audit: Reclaiming Your Mental Real Estate

There are 168 hours in a week. If you are an "option," a staggering percentage of those hours is likely spent in "Unpaid Emotional Labor." You are working a full-time job for a company that isn't paying you.

Exercise: The Solo Equity Map

1. **Audit:** Track your time for three days. Be honest. How many hours are spent on *his* reality (checking his socials, talking about him with friends, waiting for him to reply, staring at a blank screen)?
2. **Analysis:** Now, how many hours are spent on *your* reality (your career growth, your physical health, your genuine joy, your creative projects)?
3. **Reallocation:** Aim for a "Priority Ratio" of 90/10. 90% of your mental and physical energy must be directed toward the life you are building alone. This creates a "Moat" around your peace. If he wants access to that 10%, he has to prove he is worth the interruption.

The "High-Value" Exit: Why Solo Joy is the Ultimate Leverage

Paradoxically, the moment you stop needing a man to make your life feel "real" is the moment you become truly "high-value." This isn't a tactic to "get him back"; it is a transformation that makes his return irrelevant.

A woman who loves her life alone is dangerous to a low-effort man because she cannot be bought with crumbs. She cannot be manipulated with "maybe." When your life is full, the "cost" of letting a man in becomes much higher. You begin to look at a potential partner and ask: *"Is his presence better than my peace? Is his conversation more interesting than my book? Is his consistency better than my solitude?"* If the answer is no, you walk away without hesitation. You aren't walking into a void; you are walking back to a life you already love. This is the "Strong Alternative" that economists talk about in negotiations. If you have a great alternative (your solo life), you have all the power.

The Spiritual Dimension of the Solo Life

Beyond the psychology and biology, there is a spiritual reclamation in being alone. It is the practice of **Internal Validation**. In the Option Cycle, you were looking for someone to tell you that you were "good," "worthy," and "enough."

When you build a life alone, you realize that those words can only ever come from you. You become your own witness. You see your own growth, you celebrate your own wins, and you comfort your own sorrows. This self-witnessing is the highest form of love. It is the love that never leaves, never ghosts, and never makes you an option.

Conclusion: You Are the Destination

You have spent a lifetime believing that love is something you find "out there," in the hands of a man who might eventually choose you. You thought of yourself as a traveler and him as the home you were trying to reach.

The truth of Part 5, and the truth of this entire book, is that the most important choice has already been made. By finding your voice, moving away from those who don't show up, leaning on your support system, and building a life you love alone, you have chosen *yourself*.

You are no longer an option on someone else's list. You are the destination. You are the priority. You are finally, fully, home.

REFLECTION EXERCISES

CHAPTERS 18 TO 21

This reflection section is all about the reconstruction of your identity.

You are moving from a reactive state, where your mood, your schedule, and your self-worth were dictated by his "pings", to a proactive state. This is the stage where you stop being an "option" and start being the "main character."

Chapter 18: Finding Your Voice

The Objective: To transition from "social fawning" (silencing yourself to maintain attachment) to "authentic resonance". You will practice the physical and psychological mechanics of being heard.

Part A: The "Swallowed Words" Archive

Silence in a lopsided relationship is a form of slow-motion self-erasure. In Chapter 18, we discussed the "Cool Girl" trap, the pressure to be low-maintenance by never speaking up.

1. **The Catalog of Suppression:** Look back over the last six months. List ten specific instances where you felt a "no" in your gut but said "yes" with your lips, or where you had a grievance but swallowed it.
    - *Example:* "He showed up two hours late, and I said 'It's fine, I was busy anyway' instead of 'My time is valuable and this hurt my feelings.'"
2. **The Somatic Signature:** For each instance, describe the physical sensation in your body. Did your stomach flip? Did you feel a hot flush in your cheeks? Did your throat feel like it was closing?
    - *Note:* This is your **Ambiance of Truth**. Your body tells the truth even when your mouth lies. Learning to recognize these signals is the first step to reclaiming your voice.
3. **The "Safety" Myth:** What was the specific catastrophe you were trying to prevent by staying silent? (e.g., "If I tell him I'm hurt, he will think I'm high-drama and stop calling.") Write down the fear, then ask: "Is a relationship where I cannot speak my truth actually 'safe'?"

Part B: The Vagal Tone and Vocal Authority Workshop

Your voice is controlled by the **Vagus Nerve**. When you are in a "freeze" or "fawn" state, your vocal cords tighten, making your voice thin, high, or shaky. To reclaim your voice, you must reclaim your biology.

- **Exercise 1: The Low-Frequency Hum.** Sit comfortably. Place one hand on your chest and one on your throat. Inhale deeply into your belly. On the exhale, make a low "Mmm" sound. Try to feel the vibration move from your throat down into your chest. This "vocal toning" stimulates the ventral vagal complex, signaling to your brain that it is safe to speak.
- **Exercise 2: The Power Posture.** Stand with your feet shoulder-width apart. Imagine a string pulling the crown of your head toward the ceiling. Speak three sentences about your day in this posture. Notice how much more "weight" your voice has when your airway is open and your spine is aligned.

- **Exercise 3: Mirror Work.** Look into your own eyes. Say: *"I am allowed to have needs that are inconvenient for others."* Repeat this 10 times. Observe how your face changes. Do you look apologetic? Do you look defiant? Aim for a look of "neutral authority".

Part C: The "FAST" Communication Lab

Using the DBT skill **FAST** (Fair, No Apologies, Stick to Values, Truthful), rewrite the following "Option" phrases into "Priority" phrases:

The "Option" Phrase	The "FAST" (Priority) Phrase
"I'm sorry, I know you're busy, but could we maybe talk?"	"I have something important to discuss. Are you free at 6:00 PM?"
"It's okay that you forgot my birthday, I know work is crazy."	"I felt disappointed that you forgot my birthday. Celebrating is important to me."
"Just checking in! No pressure at all, but let me know about Friday."	"I'm finalizing my weekend plans. Let me know by noon tomorrow if we're on for Friday."

Chapter 19: Moving Away

The Objective: To enact the "Let Them" theory by physically and digitally withdrawing your energy from a person who does not "show up."

Part A: The "Effort Equilibrium" Map

In Chapter 19, we talked about moving away from "No-Show" partners. Use this visual exercise to see the reality of your current investment.

1. **The Investment Circle:** Draw a large circle. This represents 100% of the emotional energy in the relationship.
2. **The Divide:** Shade in the portion that represents *your* effort (initiating texts, planning dates, emotional support). Now, shade in a different color the portion representing *his* effort.
3. **The Visualization:** If your circle is 90% one color and 10% the other, you are not in a relationship; you are in a solo performance.

4. **The "Ghost" Archetype:** Identify which "No-Show" archetype he fits: The Digital Ghost, The Crisis-Only Partner, or The Vague Planner. Write down three specific "No-Show" events from the last month.

Part B: The Digital and Emotional "Clean Room"

Moving away is difficult because our phones provide "digital proximity." Your brain thinks he is "right here" because his name is on your screen.

- **The Mute/Restrict Protocol:** For the next 21 days (the time it takes to begin breaking a dopamine loop), mute his stories and posts. If you use an app like Instagram, "Restrict" him so his messages go to a separate folder.
- **The Notification Silence:** Turn off "Read Receipts" and "Last Seen" statuses. This removes the "surveillance" aspect of the relationship that keeps your amygdala in a state of high alert.
- **The 24-Hour Buffer:** Before responding to any low-effort text (e.g., "Hey," "U up?"), wait 24 hours. During that time, ask yourself: "Am I responding because I want to, or because I'm afraid he'll disappear if I don't?"

Part C: Reclaiming Your Time and Calendar

We often live in a state of "pending." We don't book trips or classes because "he might want to do something that weekend."

1. **The "Pending" Audit:** List three things you have postponed or avoided doing because you were waiting for him to initiate or confirm.
2. **The Commitment:** Book one of those things *today*. Pay for it. Make it non-refundable.
3. **The "Firm Date" Rule:** From now on, any plan without a specific Time, Date, and Location is not a plan; it is a "maybe." And you do not wait for "maybes."

Chapter 20: Leaning on Your Support System

The Objective: To replace "co-dependency" with "healthy inter-dependency" by re-engaging with the people who actually value you.

Part A: The Social Portfolio Audit

In Chapter 20, we discussed the four pillars of a support system. List the people in your life who fit these roles:

- **The Emotional Anchor (Safety):** ______________________________
- **The Truth-Teller (Accountability):** ____________________________
- **The Distraction Architect (Fun):** ______________________________
- **The Mentor (Aspiration):** ____________________________________

Reflect: Are you putting 90% of your energy into a man who isn't even on this list, while ignoring the people who are?

Part B: The "Vulnerability Vulnerability" Exercise

We often hide our struggles in an "Option" relationship because we don't want our friends to tell us to leave. This isolation keeps you stuck.

1. **The Disclosure:** Choose one person from your "Truth-Teller" list. Tell them the honest, unvarnished truth about a recent "breadcrumb" or "no-show" event.
2. **The Rule:** Do not make excuses for him. Do not say "but he's been stressed at work." Just state the facts: "He said he would call at 8:00, and he didn't call until the next day."
3. **The Support Request:** Ask your friend: "Can you check in on me this Friday to make sure I'm not just sitting at home waiting for him?"

Part C: The Biology of Belonging

Research shows that physical presence with safe friends lowers cortisol.

- **The Action:** Schedule a "No-Phone" outing with a friend. For two hours, leave your phones in a bag.
- **The Observation:** Notice how your nervous system feels after 60 minutes of uninterrupted human eye contact and conversation. Does the "craving" for his digital attention feel less intense? This is **Co-Regulation** in action.

Chapter 21: Build a Life That You Love Alone

The Objective: To cultivate "Autonomous Joy" so that your life feels like a vibrant, finished masterpiece, not a "work in progress" waiting for a man to provide the final brushstroke.

Part A: The "Sanctuary" and "Sovereignty" Audit

Your home and your habits should reflect your worth.

1. **The Sanctuary Check:** Look around your living space. Is it set up for *your* comfort, or are you keeping it in a "guest-ready" state for a man who rarely visits? Buy the plants, the art, or the furniture that *you* love, even if he wouldn't "get it."
2. **The Solo Ritual:** Identify one thing you love to do but usually save for "date nights" (e.g., going to a specific restaurant, watching a certain genre of film, taking a long bath with expensive salts).
3. **The Execution:** Do that thing alone this week. Document how it feels to be the source of your own luxury.

Part B: The Mastery and "Flow State" Challenge

Nothing builds self-esteem like competence. When you are an "option," your mind is often "scattered." Mastery requires "gathering" your focus.

- **The Activity:** Choose a skill that requires total concentration (e.g., learning a difficult song on an instrument, complex cooking, a 1000-piece puzzle, high-intensity interval training).
- **The Science:** When you enter a "Flow State," your brain shuts down the **Medial Prefrontal Cortex** (the part responsible for self-monitoring and rumination). You literally *cannot* worry about him while you are in "Flow."
- **The Reflection:** After 30 minutes of this activity, check in with yourself. Do you feel more powerful? Does he feel smaller?

Part C: The "Let Them" Manifesto

Write out your "Let Them" rules for the next month:

- *If he wants to go silent,* ***let him.***
- *If he wants to spend his weekend without me,* ***let him.***

- *If he wants to miss out on the incredible woman I am becoming,* ***let him.***

Final Synthesis Question: If you were the woman of your own dreams, the most prioritized, respected, and loved version of yourself, what is the very first thing you would do for yourself tomorrow morning?

Now, go do it.

PART SIX

LIVING AS A PRIORITY

CHAPTER 22

IDENTIFY WARNING SIGNS BEFORE YOU GET HOOKED

The most effective way to escape the "Option Cycle" is to never step onto the carousel in the first place.

By the time you are three months deep, your brain is marinating in a cocktail of **Oxytocin**, **Dopamine**, and **Vasopressin**. At that stage, your logical brain (the **Prefrontal Cortex**) is essentially out to lunch, leaving the emotional centers of your brain to run the show. This is why "leaving" feels like a withdrawal from a physical drug, because, biologically, it is.

Chapter 22 is about the **Discernment Phase**. It is about the first three to five dates, the critical window where you still have the clarity to walk away without a shattered heart. To live as a priority, you must become a high-level gatekeeper. You must learn to identify the "Option-Maker" while he is still a stranger, before his "potential" becomes your "obsession."

The Biology of the "Gut Feeling": Neuroception

Before a red flag ever registers as a conscious thought, your body has already processed it. This is a process called **Neuroception**, a term coined by Dr. Stephen Porges. It is your nervous system's subconscious ability to detect "threat" or "safety" in the environment and in people.

When you are on a first date with a man who will eventually treat you as an option, your neuroception often sends subtle signals:

- A slight tightening in your solar plexus.
- A fleeting sense of "performance" or "on-ness" from him.
- A sudden urge to "fill the silence" or prove your worth.
- A subtle "buzzing" of anxiety that you misinterpret as "chemistry".

In the "Option Cycle", we are taught to ignore these signals in favor of "giving him a chance". Living as a priority means honoring the signal the first time it fires. If your body feels like it's in a "high-alert" state around someone you barely know, that isn't a spark; it's a siren.

The "Big Five" Early Warning Signs

An "Option-Maker" usually reveals himself within the first 10 hours of interaction. He relies on specific behavioral patterns to bypass your defenses. Recognising these early is your superpower.

1. The Fast-Forwarder (Love Bombing Lite)

He speaks in the "Future Tense" almost immediately. Within two dates, he's talking about trips you'll take in the summer, or how he's "never felt this way before".

- **The Trap:** It feels like a priority dynamic because he's giving you so much attention.
- **The Reality:** This is **Intensity**, not **Intimacy**. Intimacy is built over time through consistent action. Intensity is a tool used to create a quick "bond" so that when he eventually pulls back, you are already "hooked" on the high.

2. The "Victim" Narrative

Pay close attention to how he speaks about his "crazy" exes or the people who have "wronged" him.

- **The Warning:** If every woman in his past was "unhinged," "needy," or "difficult," he is likely an **Accountability Dodger**.
- **The Future Projection:** Eventually, *you* will be the "crazy ex" he tells the next woman about. A priority man takes responsibility for his role in past failures.

3. The Boundary Tester

He pushes small boundaries early to see how much you will "edit" yourself to accommodate him.

- **Examples:** He asks for a last-minute date when you already mentioned you were busy. He makes a "joke" that is slightly disparaging to see if you'll laugh or call him out. He pushes for physical intimacy before you've indicated you're ready.
- **The Diagnostic:** If he reacts with annoyance, "guilt-tripping," or a "joke" when you say "no," he is not looking for a priority; he is looking for a person he can manage.

4. The "Mystery Man" (Vague Scheduling)

He is a master of the "Soft Plan." He uses phrases like "Let's hang out this weekend" or "I'll see what my schedule looks like."

- **The Red Flag:** He refuses to give a specific time or location until the very last minute.
- **The Logic:** This keeps his options open. He is essentially waiting to see if a "better" offer (or a different option) comes along before he commits his time to you.

5. The "Inconsistent Ping"

He is "all over you" for 48 hours and then goes radio silent for three days without explanation.

- **The Biological Impact:** This triggers **Intermittent Reinforcement** (as discussed in Chapter 19). Your brain becomes hyper-focused on the next "ping," creating an artificial sense of importance around him.

Red Flags vs. Beige Flags vs. Deal-Breakers

To be a discerning gatekeeper, you must categorize what you see. Use the following table as a decoder:

Category	Definition	Example	Action
Red Flag	A sign of a toxic or manipulative character trait.	Love bombing, lying, mocking you, extreme jealousy.	**Exit Immediately.** Do not pass go.
Beige Flag	A quirk or behavior that isn't harmful but might be a compatibility mismatch.	He has "boring" hobbies, he's a slow texter but consistent, he's picky about food.	**Observe.** Communicate your needs and see if he adjusts.
Deal-Breaker	A fundamental misalignment in values or life goals.	He doesn't want kids (you do), he lives 5 hours away, different religious requirements.	**Friendly Exit.** Respect your own non-negotiables.

The "Entrance Exam": 3 Questions to Ask Yourself After Date Two

Most women spend the first few dates asking, *"Does he like me?"* To live as a priority, you must flip the script and ask, *"Is he qualified to be in my life?"*

1. **"How does my body feel when I'm *not* with him?"**
    - o If you feel peaceful and energized, it's a good sign.
    - o If you feel anxious, checking your phone every five minutes, and "wound up," your nervous system is detecting a "No-Show" threat.
2. **"Did he ask me a single deep question about my life?"**
    - o Option-Makers often talk about themselves or stick to "flirty" surface-level banter. They don't actually want to know *you*; they want a mirror to reflect their own greatness.

3. **"Is he a 'Word' man or a 'Work' man?"**
   - Does he say he's a "great communicator" while taking 10 hours to reply? Does he say he's "looking for something serious" while keeping his plans vague? Trust the **Work (Action)**, never the **Word**.

Self-Gaslighting: The Saboteur of Discernment

The biggest obstacle to identifying warning signs isn't him, it's **you**. When we like someone, we engage in **Confirmation Bias**. We look for reasons why he *is* a priority and ignore the evidence that he is an "Option-Maker."

You might say:

- *"He's just really busy with work."*
- *"He probably just hasn't had a good relationship example."*
- *"He was so sweet on the first date, maybe I'm being too sensitive."*

Stop. This is self-gaslighting. Discernment requires you to look at the **Mean Behavior**, not the **Peak Behavior**. If he is sweet 20% of the time and inconsistent 80% of the time, he is an inconsistent man. Period.

Conclusion: The Power of the "Early No"

There is a strange, intoxicating power in saying "no" to a man who shows you a red flag on date three. It feels like a win for your future self. When you identify a warning sign and choose to walk away before you are "hooked," you are reinforcing the neural pathways of self-worth.

You are telling your brain: *"I would rather be alone and peaceful than 'chosen' by someone who makes me feel small."* This is the foundation of Part 6. By the time we get to the next chapter, you will learn how to show up so authentically that the "Option-Makers" are naturally filtered out by your very presence.

CHAPTER 23

BE YOUR REAL SELF FROM THE FIRST DATE

The greatest irony of the "Option Cycle" is that we often try to escape it by becoming the most "palatable" version of ourselves. We think that if we are perfectly "chill," effortlessly beautiful, and endlessly understanding, we will finally be the one he chooses to promote to "Priority."

We call this **Impression Management**, but in reality, it is a high-stakes performance. You are essentially auditioning for a role in a play you didn't write, for a director who isn't even paying attention.

Chapter 23 is about the power of **Radical Authenticity**. To live as a priority, you must stop trying to be the woman he wants and start being the woman you actually are, from the very first "Hello." This isn't just about "being yourself"; it is a strategic, biological filtering mechanism that ensures you never waste time on a man who is only looking for a surface-level option.

The "Cool Girl" Trap: Why Performance Fails

Gillian Flynn described the "Cool Girl" in her novel *Gone Girl*, the woman who is hot, brilliant, funny, and most importantly, never gets angry, never complains, and is always "down for whatever".

Many women enter the first date wearing the Cool Girl mask. They think that by being "low maintenance", they are showing high value. However, from a neurological perspective, this is a disaster for two reasons:

1. **Cognitive Load:** When you are performing, your **Prefrontal Cortex** is working overtime to monitor your speech, your posture, and your reactions. You aren't actually *present* for the date; you are a technician managing a broadcast. You miss the subtle red flags (Chapter 22) because you are too busy checking your own "signal."
2. **The "False Positive" Attachment:** If he likes the "Cool Girl", he isn't liking *you*. He is liking a curated avatar. This creates a terrifying sense of insecurity: you know that the moment you show a real emotion (anger, sadness, a boundary), the connection might collapse. You have built a house on sand.

The Priority Mindset: A woman who knows she is a priority doesn't need to "win" the date. She is there to see if *he* is a good fit for *her* life.

Authenticity as a Biological Filter

When you show up as your real self, complete with your opinions, your boundaries, and your quirks, you are performing a "Stress Test" on the connection.

Authenticity is a filter that saves you months of heartbreak.

- **The "Option-Maker"** is threatened by a woman with a strong sense of self. He wants someone he can mold, someone whose boundaries are "flexible," and someone who is too "polite" to call out his inconsistency. When you are real from Day One, he will usually filter himself out. He will find you "too much," "intense," or "difficult." **Let him.**
- **The "Priority Man"** is attracted to clarity. He is looking for a partner, not a project. He finds your honesty refreshing and your boundaries attractive because they indicate self-respect.

What "Being Your Real Self" Actually Looks Like

There is a common misconception that "being real" means "trauma dumping" or sharing your deepest insecurities over appetizers. That isn't authenticity; that is an **Anxious Attachment** play for premature intimacy.

Real authenticity is about **Alignment**. It is ensuring that your external actions match your internal values.

1. Own Your Opinions

If he says he loves a movie that you found boring, don't nod and agree to be "likable." Say, *"Really? I actually struggled with the pacing. I prefer stories that are a bit more character-driven."* * **The Goal:** You are showing him that you have an internal world that doesn't bend to his.

2. Don't Hide Your Standards

If the conversation turns to what you're looking for, don't say "Oh, I'm just seeing where things go" (unless that's true). If you want a long-term partner, say it.

- **The Phrase:** *"I'm at a stage in my life where I'm looking for a consistent, meaningful connection. I enjoy my life alone, so I'm only looking for something that adds to it."* * **The Effect:** This immediately scares off the "Casual King" and signals to the "Priority Man" that you are a high-value woman with a clear direction.

3. Let Your "Weird" Show

If you have a strange hobby, a dorky sense of humor, or a specific way you like your coffee, don't hide it to seem "normal."

- **The Logic:** You want to be loved for the parts of you that are unique. The sooner he sees them, the sooner you know if he's your "person".

The Power of "Selective Vulnerability"

Authenticity requires vulnerability, but it should be **earned vulnerability**. Think of it as a house: you don't let a stranger into your bedroom on the first day, but you should let them through the front door.

Don't (Trauma Dumping)	Do (Selective Vulnerability)
"My ex was a narcissist who ruined my life and I have major trust issues."	"I've learned a lot from my past relationships about the importance of communication and consistency."
"I'm so nervous right now, I usually mess up first dates."	"I'll be honest, I'm feeling a little bit of first-date jitters, but I'm really happy to be here."
"I need someone to choose me because I'm tired of being an option."	"I value my time, so I really appreciate it when someone is intentional and clear about their interest."

Breaking the "Pleaser" Neural Pathway

If you have been an "option" for a long time, your brain has likely built a strong neural pathway for **People Pleasing**. When you feel a "threat" to the connection (e.g., a moment of disagreement), your **Amygdala** fires, urging you to apologize or soften your stance to keep him "happy."

To break this, you must practice **The Pause.**

When you feel the urge to "perform" or "please":

1. **Breathe:** Take a three-second inhale. This moves you from the Sympathetic (Fight/Flight) system to the Parasympathetic (Rest/Digest) system.
2. **Observe:** Ask yourself, *"Am I saying this because it's true, or because I want him to like me?"*
3. **Correct:** If it's not true, don't say it. Silence is better than a performative lie.

Conclusion: You Are the Prize, Not the Applicant

When you show up as your real self, you are no longer an "applicant" trying to get "hired" for the role of girlfriend. You are the **CEO** of your own life, conducting an interview.

If you are "too much" for him, he is not enough for you. If your honesty makes him uncomfortable, his inconsistency would have made you miserable. By being your real self from the first date, you aren't just finding a partner—you are protecting the woman you worked so hard to reclaim in Part 5.

CHAPTER 24

VALUE CONSISTENCY OVER A SUDDEN SPARK

We have been sold a lie about the "Spark."

Hollywood, romance novels, and pop songs have conditioned us to believe that if the first date doesn't feel like a high-speed chase or a lightning strike, it isn't "the one". We look for that dizzying, nauseating, electric rush of adrenaline and call it "chemistry." That spark is often nothing more than your nervous system sounding an alarm.

Chapter 24 is about the Great Rewiring. To move from being an option to being a priority, you must stop being a "spark-chaser" and start being a "consistency-collector." You must learn to distinguish between the **anxiety of the unknown** and the **safety of the known**.

The Neurochemistry of the Spark: Why It's Dangerous

When you meet someone and feel that immediate, overwhelming "spark," your brain isn't necessarily finding a soulmate. It is likely experiencing a massive surge of **Dorepinephrine** and **Dopamine**.

This chemical cocktail is the same one released during gambling or drug use. It creates a state of **Hyper-Arousal**.

- **The Dopamine Spike:** This makes you obsess. You can't eat, you can't sleep, and you are constantly checking your phone.
- **The Cortisol Rise:** The "butterflies" in your stomach are actually a mild stress response. Your body is in "Fight or Flight" because it doesn't yet know if this person is a friend or a predator.

If you have a history of being treated as an option, your brain might misinterpret this stress as "excitement." You have been conditioned to believe that love is something you have to "win" or "chase," so when a man feels elusive or mysterious (creating a spark of uncertainty), your brain locks on. You aren't attracted to *him*; you are attracted to the **dopamine loop** created by his unpredictability.

Consistency: The Quiet Priority

Consistency is the ultimate "green flag," but it rarely feels like a lightning bolt. Consistency feels like a warm bath. It feels like a long exhale. It feels like **safety**.

In a priority dynamic, consistency is the "Work" that supports the "Word." While the "Option-Maker" uses the spark to distract you from his lack of follow-through, the "Priority Man" uses his actions to build a foundation of trust.

The Biological Impact of Consistency

When a partner is consistent, meaning they call when they say they will, they show up on time, and their mood is predictable, your nervous system enters a state of **Ventral Vagal Regulation**.

- **Oxytocin Release:** Unlike the "hit" of dopamine, oxytocin is the hormone of long-term bonding and calm. It lowers blood pressure and reduces anxiety.

- **Serotonin Stabilization:** Consistency keeps your mood stable. You don't have the "crashes" that follow the high of a spark-filled date with an inconsistent man.

The "Predictability Paradox": Why We Think Consistency is Boring

One of the hardest parts of reclaiming the woman within is admitting that, at first, a consistent man might feel "boring".

This is the **Predictability Paradox**. Because there is no "chase," there is no "threat," and because there is no threat, there is no adrenaline. Also, because we have been trained to equate adrenaline with love, we think the lack of it means "no chemistry."

> "If you meet someone and your heart hammers and your knees knock, that's not 'The One.' That's a biological warning. The person who makes you feel calm, the person who makes you feel like you can finally take a nap, that is your priority."

To value consistency, you must reframe your definition of "boring":

- **Boring** is actually **Reliable**.
- **Boring** means you don't have to spend three hours in a group chat decoding his last text.
- **Boring** means you can focus on your career, your hobbies, and your friends because your relationship isn't a full-time job of "crisis management."

The Consistency Scorecard: The First 90 Days

To live as a priority, you must stop looking at the "Peak Moments" and start looking at the **Average Moments**. Use the following metrics to evaluate a man's consistency in the early stages:

Metric	The Option-Maker (The Spark)	The Priority Man (Consistency)
Communication	Random bursts of intensity followed by days of silence.	Steady, predictable cadence. You know when you'll hear from him.
Scheduling	"Let's hang out sometime." Late-night invites.	"Are you free Thursday at 7:00? I'll make a reservation."
Follow-Through	Makes big promises he "forgets" or "gets too busy" for.	If he says it, it happens. If it can't happen, he tells you early.
Emotional Tone	Hot and cold. You never know which version of him you'll get.	Stable. He is the same person on Tuesday that he was on Saturday.

Rewiring Your Attraction: From Chaos to Calm

If you are addicted to the spark, you can actually retrain your brain to find consistency attractive. This is a process of **Neuroplasticity**.

1. **Acknowledge the Withdrawal:** When you start dating a consistent man, you *will* miss the dopamine rush. Don't mistake this withdrawal for a "lack of connection." Tell yourself: *"My brain is just missing the chaos. I am choosing peace instead."*
2. **Focus on Mastery:** Instead of looking for a "hit" of excitement, look for "Mastery." Notice how well he handles a conflict, how he treats a waiter, or how he follows through on a small detail. Find beauty in his competence.
3. **The "Slow Burn" Visualization:** Imagine a fire. A flash-fire of dry brush burns out in minutes and leaves only ash. A slow-burning log provides heat for the entire night. Which one do you want to build a home around?

The Spark as "Recognition"

Sometimes, the spark we feel is actually **Recognition**. If you grew up in a household where love was inconsistent or had to be earned, your brain is "wired" to recognize that specific type of stress as "love."

When you meet a man who triggers that old anxiety, your brain says, *"I know this! This is home!"* This is why we often choose the same type of man over and over again. To value consistency is to reject the "familiar-unhealthy" in favor of the "unfamiliar-healthy." It requires you to be brave enough to be "bored" until your heart learns a new language.

Conclusion: You Deserve the Glow

The spark is a sprint; consistency is a marathon. An "Option-Maker" can maintain a spark for a few weeks, but only a "Priority Man" can maintain consistency for a lifetime.

When you stop chasing the lightning and start valuing the hearth, your entire life changes. You move from a state of **Relational Uncertainty** to **Relational Security**. You stop wondering "where you stand" because his consistent actions have already told you. You realize that you don't need a man to "set you on fire"; you need a man who keeps the fire burning so you can finally rest.

CHAPTER 25

TEST FOR REAL INTEREST INSTEAD OF VAGUE HOPES

We are all guilty of it. We see a man not for who he is, but for who he *could* be. We fall in love with his "potential," his "vibe," or the way he looked at us that one time three weeks ago. This is the domain of **Vague Hope**.

Vague hope is the fuel that keeps the "Option Cycle" running. It is the mental gymnastics we perform to turn a late-night "Thinking of you" text into a sign of deep emotional longing. It is the "maybe" that prevents us from seeing the "no".

To live as a priority, you must become a scientist of your own life. You must stop being a consumer of fantasies and start being a collector of data. Chapter 25 is about the **"Load Test"**, the intentional process of putting weight on a connection to see if it's built on a foundation of real interest or the hollow scaffolding of vague hope.

The Neurobiology of Hope: The "Dopamine of the Maybe"

Why is it so hard to let go of a man who gives us so little? The answer lies in the way our brains process uncertainty.

In the world of neuroscience, **Intermittent Reinforcement** is the strongest way to condition behavior. If a lab rat gets a pellet of food every time it presses a lever, it eventually gets bored. However, if it only gets a pellet *sometimes* and at *random* intervals, it will press that lever until it collapses from exhaustion.

When a man is inconsistent, your brain creates a high-voltage dopamine loop. You aren't addicted to *him*; you are addicted to the **hope** that the next time you press the "lever" (check your phone), you'll get the "pellet" (his attention). Vague hope is literally a chemical high. To break the cycle, you have to choose the "boring" reality over the "exciting" uncertainty.

Vague Hope vs. Real Interest: The Decoder

Before we test, we must define. You have spent months, perhaps years, blurring these lines. It is time to draw them in permanent ink.

Feature	Vague Hope (The Option)	Real Interest (The Priority)
Language	Uses "Future Tense" without "Calendar Tense." (e.g., "We should go to Paris one day.")	Uses "Specific Tense." (e.g., "I checked my schedule, are you free for dinner Thursday at 7:00?")
Effort	Low-stakes "Pings" (Instagram likes, memes, late-night texts).	High-stakes "Presence" (Phone calls, planned dates, showing up when it's inconvenient).

Feature	Vague Hope (The Option)	Real Interest (The Priority)
Transparency	You feel like a detective trying to solve a mystery.	You feel like a partner being kept in the loop.
Response to "No"	He disappears or makes you feel "difficult" for having boundaries.	He adjusts and respects the boundary to keep the connection.
Integration	You are a secret. You haven't met his inner circle.	You are a fixture. You know his friends, his family, or at least his daily world.

The "Load Test": Putting Weight on the Connection

In engineering, a "Load Test" involves placing weight on a structure to see if it can handle the pressure it was designed for. In dating, we often do the opposite: we make ourselves "light" and "easy" so the structure never has to prove its strength. We don't ask for what we want because we are afraid it will "scare him off".

The Priority Truth: If a man is "scared off" by a reasonable request for consistency or clarity, he was never going to be a Priority Man anyway. You haven't "lost" him; you have successfully diagnosed him.

How to Conduct a Load Test

A load test is a clear, polite, and firm request for an action that requires him to choose your comfort over his convenience.

1. The Scheduling Test

- **The Scenario:** He texts you on Friday night at 9:00 PM to "hang out."
- **The Vague Hope Response:** "Sure! I was just finishing a movie anyway." (You drop your life to accommodate his lack of planning.)

- **The Load Test:** "I'd love to see you, but I don't do last-minute plans on the weekend. If you'd like to take me out, I'm free next Tuesday or Wednesday. Let me know by Sunday if either of those work for you."
- **The Result:** A man with **Real Interest** will apologize and book the Tuesday date. An **Option-Maker** will "get busy" or tell you you're "too intense".

2. The Communication Test

- **The Scenario:** He goes silent for three days, then pings you with a "Hey."
- **The Vague Hope Response:** "Hey! How was your week??" (You ignore the silence to keep the peace.)
- **The Load Test:** "Hey. Honestly, I'm a woman who values consistent communication. When you go quiet for days, I lose interest. I'm looking for someone who is a bit more present."
- **The Result:** This puts the "weight" of the interaction on his shoulders. He must either step up or step out.

The Five Essential "Interest Audits"

To move from hope to data, you must perform these five audits regularly in the first 90 days of any connection.

1. The Proactivity Audit

Who is doing the heavy lifting? Keep a mental (or physical) log of the last five dates. Who initiated the conversation? Who chose the location? Who confirmed the time? If you are the "project manager" of the relationship, you are an option. A Priority Man manages the connection because he is afraid of losing it.

2. The Visibility Audit

Does the world know you exist? Real interest is proud. It wants to integrate you into its life. If you have been seeing a man for two months and you haven't met a single friend, or if he "forgets" to introduce you to someone he runs into on the street, you are a "Hidden Option".

3. The Vulnerability Audit

When you share something real, a struggle at work, a family issue, a fear, how does he respond?

- **Real Interest:** He leans in, asks follow-up questions, and validates the feeling.
- **Vague Hope:** He changes the subject. He makes a joke. Sends an emoji. He doesn't want the "weight" of your reality; he only wants the "lightness" of your company.

4. The "Inconvenience" Audit

Interest is easy when everything is perfect. Real interest is proven when things get difficult. If you get a flat tire, if you're sick, or if you're having a bad day, does he show up? A man who only wants an "Option" will disappear the moment the "vibe" becomes "work".

5. The Consistency Audit (The 3-Day Rule)

Look at his behavior over a 72-hour period. Is it predictable? If you can't predict when you'll hear from him or when you'll see him again, you are living in a "Dopamine Slot Machine". Real interest provides a steady rhythm.

Interpreting the Data: The "No" is a Gift

The scariest part of testing for real interest is the possibility of a "negative result." We are so afraid of the "No" that we prefer the "Maybe."

But in the economy of your life, a **Fast No** is worth more than a **Long Maybe**.

- A **Long Maybe** wastes your time, drains your energy, and keeps you from meeting a man who would treat you as a priority.
- A **Fast No** gives you your life back. It is the "Negative Predictive Value" that allows you to close the door and move toward an open one.

> "The truth will set you free, but first it will make you miserable." - James Baldwin

When you conduct these tests, you must be prepared to accept the data. If the bridge breaks under the load, do not try to tape it back together. Thank the test for showing you the structural weakness before you moved your entire heart onto that bridge.

The Power of the "Observational Pause"

Sometimes, the best test is to do absolutely nothing. We call this the **Observational Pause**.

If you have been the one driving the relationship, stop. Don't text first. Don't suggest the next date. Don't "check in".

- This is not a "game." This is an **Information Gathering Mission**.
- You are creating a vacuum. **Real Interest** will rush in to fill that vacuum because it doesn't want the connection to die. **Vague Hope** will allow the vacuum to stay empty because it was never invested in the first place.

Conclusion: Trust Your Data, Not Your Dreams

Vague hope is a beautiful dream, but you cannot build a life in a dream. You are a woman who deserves a love that is documented in actions, not just whispered in possibilities.

By testing for real interest, you are protecting the "Woman Within" that you reclaimed in Part 5. You are telling the world that your time is a finite, precious resource, and you do not spend it on "maybes." When you stop hoping and start observing, you stop being an option. You become the woman who chooses reality, and in that reality, you are always the priority.

REFLECTION EXERCISES

CHAPTERS 22 TO 25

Welcome to the implementation phase. If the previous chapters were about healing and rebuilding your internal foundation, these exercises are about the "stress test". You are taking your reclaimed self back into the world of connection, but this time, you are carrying a shield of data and a sword of discernment.

The goal of these exercises is to move you from **Intuition** (feeling something is off) to **Action** (doing something about it). We are going to rewire your dating "operating system" so that you no longer attract or tolerate "Option-Makers". These exercises are intended to be done while you are actively dating or reflecting on a very recent connection.

Chapter 22: The Gatekeeper's Audit

The Objective: To refine your "Neuroception" (gut feeling) and identify the specific red flags of an Option-Maker before your heart overrides your head.

Part A: The Red Flag Post-Mortem

Think back to the last time you were treated as an option. We are going to look for the "ghosts" of that relationship in your current or future dating life.

1. **The "Day One" Signal:** Close your eyes and think back to the first three dates with that person. What was the *very first* thing that made you pause, even for a second? (e.g., He mentioned an ex-girlfriend, he was 15 minutes late without a text, he made a joke at your expense).
2. **The Justification:** What did you tell yourself to "explain away" that signal? Write down the exact sentence. (e.g., "He's just stressed at work," "I'm probably being too sensitive.")
3. **The Pattern Match:** Look at the "Big Five" warning signs from Chapter 22 (The Fast-Forwarder, The Victim, The Boundary Tester, The Mystery Man, The Inconsistent Ping). Which one was his "primary move"?

Part B: The Neuroception Journal

For the next three people you interact with (dating or otherwise), perform a **Somatic Scan**.

- **During the Interaction:** Check in with your body.
  - o Is your breath shallow or deep?
  - o Are your shoulders near your ears?
  - o Do you feel a sense of "urgency" to impress them?
- **The Post-Date Scorecard:**
  - o **Calm Score (1-10):** How much did my nervous system feel "at home"?
  - o **Performance Score (1-10):** How much did I feel I was "on stage"?
  - o *Reflection:* A Priority Man will usually result in a high Calm Score and a low Performance Score. If you have a high Performance Score, your neuroception is likely detecting a "Conditional Interest" threat.

Part C: The "Victim Narrative" Decoder

The next time a man tells you about his past, use this translation table to see if he is an "Accountability Dodger."

What He Says	What It Might Actually Mean	The Follow-Up Question
"All my exes are crazy."	"I lack the self-awareness to see my role in conflict."	"That's a lot of 'crazy.' What do you think led to those dynamics?"
"I'm just not a 'labels' guy."	"I want the benefits of a relationship without the priority."	"I appreciate the honesty. What *are* you a 'guy' for?"
"My last girlfriend was so needy."	"I am emotionally unavailable and view boundaries as a burden."	"What did 'needy' look like to you?"

Chapter 23: The Authenticity Stress-Test

The Objective: To kill the "Cool Girl" once and for all and ensure that you are being loved for who you *are*, not the version of you that is "easy" to date.

Part A: The "Cool Girl" Obituary

Write a short "obituary" for the version of you that used to be "chill" and "low-maintenance" to keep a man interested.

- *Example:* "Today we lay to rest 'Chill Sarah.' She never asked for what she wanted, she pretended to like hiking when she actually hates it, and she swallowed her anger until it turned into a migraine. She is being replaced by 'Real Sarah,' who has opinions, needs, and a very limited amount of patience for BS."

Part B: The Standards Scripting Lab

One of the hardest parts of being your real self is stating your standards out loud. Practice writing these scripts until they feel like "neutral facts" rather than "confessions."

1. **Stating Your Intent (Date 1 or 2):**
   - *The Prompt:* "So, what are you looking for?"
   - *The Script:* "I'm really enjoying building my life right now, so I'm only looking for something that adds to it. I value consistency and I'm looking for a partner who is ready for a real connection. How about you?"
2. **Addressing Inconsistency (Date 3 or 4):**
   - *The Prompt:* He texts "Hey" after three days of silence.
   - *The Script:* "Hey! To be honest, I'm the kind of woman who values a steady flow of communication. I find that when it's sporadic, I lose the thread of the connection. If that's not your style, I totally understand, but it's what I need to feel interested."

Part C: The "Weirdness" Exposure

On your next date (or in your next conversation), intentionally share one "un-cool" thing about yourself.

- Share a dorky hobby.
- State a "hot take" opinion that might be unpopular.
- Order exactly what you want to eat without worrying if it's "too much" or "too messy."
- **The Observation:** Notice his reaction. Does he lean in and ask more? Or does he look judged/uncomfortable?
  - *The Data:* If he is uncomfortable with your "weird," he is not your priority. He is looking for a template, not a person.

Chapter 24: The Adrenaline vs. Peace Audit

The Objective: To rewire your attraction to favor consistency over the "spark" and to recognize the difference between "Anxious Attachment" and "Secure Connection."

Part A: The Spark-Chaser's History

List the last three people you felt an intense "spark" with.

1. How long did the "spark" last?
2. How many of those connections turned into a consistent, prioritizing relationship?

3. Looking back, was the "spark" actually **Adrenaline** (fear of loss, uncertainty, mystery) or **Safety**?

Part B: The Peace-Rating Scale

When you meet someone new, stop asking "Was there a spark?" and start using the **Peace-Rating Scale**. Rate the connection on the following (1-10):

- **Predictability:** Do I know when I'll hear from them?
- **Clarity:** Do I know how they feel about me?
- **Body Comfort:** Does my heart rate stay steady when I'm with them?
- **Mental Real Estate:** Am I spending less than 10% of my day wondering what they're thinking?

Note: If the score is high (8+) and you feel "bored," that is your signal to stay. You are in "withdrawal" from the drama. Do not leave the "boredom" until you have given it at least five dates.

Part C: The "Boring" Reframe Exercise

Take five "consistent" behaviors and reframe them from "boring" to "high-value."

The "Boring" Thought	The "High-Value" Reframe
"He texts me every morning at 8 AM. It's so predictable."	"He is reliable and prioritizes being part of my daily life."
"He already planned our date for Saturday. There's no mystery."	"He respects my time and wants to ensure he gets to see me."
"He told me he really likes me. The chase is over."	"He is emotionally mature enough to be transparent and clear."
"We just went for a walk and talked. It wasn't 'electric'."	"We are building a foundation of actual friendship and safety."

Chapter 25: The Load-Test Lab

The Objective: To stop living in "Vague Hope" and start gathering "Hard Data" through intentional requests and observations.

Part A: The "Vague Hope" Inventory

Is there someone in your life right now (or recently) who you are "hoping" will change?

1. **The Fantasy:** Write down what you *hope* will happen. (e.g., "I hope he realizes he misses me and finally commits.")
2. **The Reality:** Write down what has *actually* happened in the last 14 days. (e.g., "He liked one photo, sent one meme, and didn't ask to see me.")
3. **The Gap:** Look at the distance between the Fantasy and the Reality. That gap is where your peace is dying.

Part B: Designing Your Load-Test

Pick one area of uncertainty in your current connection and design a "Load-Test" as described in Chapter 25.

- **Scenario 1: The Scheduling Test.** If he always asks you out last-minute, your test is to say "No" to the next last-minute invite and offer a specific alternative 3 days in the future.
- **Scenario 2: The Definition Test.** If you've been "hanging out" for two months, your test is to ask: "I've really enjoyed our time, but I'm looking to move toward exclusivity. Is that something you're open to?"
- **Scenario 3: The Vulnerability Test.** Share a small, real stressor from your day. See if he offers support or if he "ghosts" the conversation until the vibe is "light" again.

The Prediction: Write down what you think he will do.

The Reality: Write down what he *actually* does.

Crucial: If he fails the test, you must accept the data. You cannot "re-test" until he passes.

Part C: The Observational Pause (The 72-Hour Vacuum)

If you are the one who usually initiates contact, commit to a 72-hour **Observational Pause**.

1. Do not text, call, or "like" any of his content for 3 full days.
2. **The Goal:** You are creating space for his "Interest" to prove itself.
3. **The Journal:** * **Hour 24:** How do you feel? (Anxious? Restless?)
    - **Hour 48:** What are you realizing about the balance of the relationship?
    - **Hour 72:** Did he fill the vacuum?
    - *The Data:* If the vacuum remains empty, he is an Option-Maker. Real interest cannot tolerate a 72-hour silence from a woman they value.

Final Synthesis: The "Priority First" 90-Day Protocol

To wrap up Part 6, you are going to create your own **90-Day Protocol**. This is your personal handbook for any new person who enters your life.

1. **The "No-Go" Zone:** List three behaviors that will result in an immediate exit, no questions asked. (e.g., Being ghosted for more than 48 hours, any disparaging comment about your goals, lying).
2. **The "Slow-Burn" Mandate:** Commit to not making any major life decisions (moving in, joint accounts, deep emotional dependence) until the 90-day mark, regardless of how "perfect" it feels.
3. **The "Village" Clause:** Commit to introducing any new partner to at least two people in your "Mirror" circle (Chapter 20) by Day 45. Their neuroception is clearer than yours right now.

Final Reflection Question:

Look at the woman you were in Chapter 1, the one waiting by the phone, decoding texts, and feeling like an option. Now look at the woman you are here, conducting load-tests, valuing peace, and standing in her truth.

Which version of you is more powerful? Which version of you is ready to be a Priority?

CONCLUSION

THE ARCHITECTURE OF THE PRIORITY LIFE

You are standing at the threshold of a new era.

If you look back at the woman who first cracked open this book, or clicked into this digital journey, you might recognize her, but you are no longer her. That woman was a resident of the "Waiting Room". She was a master of the "maybe," a professional decoder of ambiguous texts, and a reluctant expert in the art of self-abandonment. She spent her precious emotional currency on men who offered only "breadcrumbs", and she convinced herself that if she could just be a little more "chill," a little more beautiful, or a little more patient, she would finally be promoted to the status of **Priority**.

Today, that woman has retired.

This conclusion is not just a summary of the chapters you've read; it is a **Master Blueprint** for the rest of your life. We have deconstructed the biology of the trauma bond, analyzed the architecture of the "Option Cycle," and performed the "Load Tests" required to filter out the inconsistent. Now, we must discuss how to inhabit this new space: how to live not just as a woman who *wants* to be a priority, but as a woman who *is* her own primary source of value.

1. The Great Biological Rewire: From Chaos to Calm

Throughout this journey, we have leaned heavily on the science of the nervous system. We discussed how "the spark" is often just your amygdala screaming in a language you mistook for romance. We talked about the **Vagus Nerve** and how a lopsided relationship keeps you in a state of high-alert sympathetic arousal.

As you close this book, your most significant victory is the **stabilization of your baseline**.

You have moved from a "Dopamine-Addicted" state to an "Oxytocin-Grounded" state. When you no longer crave the "hit" of a text from an inconsistent man, you have achieved **Neurological Autonomy**.

The Reclaimed Woman's Maintenance:

- **The 5-Second Scan:** On any given day, check your jaw, your shoulders, and your breath. If you are tensing, ask: *"Am I reacting to a lack of external validation, or am I just tired?"*
- **The Dopamine Audit:** If you find yourself reaching for your phone to "check" on someone, pause. Redirect that energy into a **Mastery Activity** (Chapter 21). You are retraining your brain to seek satisfaction from your own competence, not his attention.

2. The Death of the "Cool Girl" and the Birth of the "Real Woman"

We must take a final moment to mourn, and celebrate, the death of the "Cool Girl".

The "Cool Girl" was a mask designed to make you palatable to men who weren't ready for the weight of a real woman. She was the one who was "down for whatever," who never asked "What are we?", and who accepted last-minute invites because she didn't want to seem "difficult."

By embracing **Radical Authenticity (Chapter 23)**, you have traded "palatability" for "integrity."

A "Real Woman" is inconvenient to an "Option-Maker." She has boundaries that don't bend for a "u up?" text at 11:00 PM. She has opinions that don't shift to match his. She has a life that is so full and vibrant that a man has to be truly exceptional to even be invited into the foyer.

Living the Truth: Never apologize for being "too much." The men who find you "too much" are simply men who are "not enough." Your intensity is a filtering mechanism. It is the fire that burns away the chaff of the "Option-Makers" so that only the "Priority Men" remain.

3. The Power of the "Early No" and the "Fast Exit"

One of the most empowering shifts you've made is understanding that **"No" is a complete sentence.** In the past, you stayed in the "Option Cycle" because you were afraid of being alone or because you felt you had "invested" too much time to leave. You fell for the **Sunk Cost Fallacy**. You thought, *"I've already spent six months on this, I might as well see it through."*

Now, you understand the **Opportunity Cost**. Every hour you spend "decoding" an inconsistent man is an hour you aren't spending on your own growth, your joy, or finding the person who will actually value you.

The New Exit Strategy:

- **The Date 3 Rule:** If a man shows a Deal-Breaker or a Red Flag (Chapter 22) by the third date, you exit. You do not try to "fix" him. You do not "give him the benefit of the doubt." You simply say: *"I've enjoyed getting to know you, but I don't think our communication styles/values are a match. I wish you the best."*
- **The "Let Them" Theory:** If he wants to be silent, **let him**. If he wants to see other people, **let him**. If he wants to be low-effort, **let him**. But you don't have to be there to witness it. You move away (Chapter 19) not out of anger, but out of self-respect.

4. The Sanctuary of the Solo Life

We spent Part 5 discussing the importance of the "Solo Life." This is perhaps the most critical pillar of the Priority Life.

The biggest threat to your progress is the fear of silence. If you are afraid to be alone with your own thoughts, you will always be tempted to "fill the gap" with a low-quality man. But when your solo life is a **Sanctuary**, you are no longer dating from a place of hunger. You are dating from a place of abundance.

The Sovereign Space: Your home should be a temple to your own taste. Your schedule should be a reflection of your own goals. Your joy should be an internal fountain, not a faucet that someone else can turn on and off.

When you are "Self-Partnered" first, a man becomes an "Addition," not a "Requirement." You stop asking, *"Does he like me?"* and start asking, *"Does he deserve a seat in this garden?"*

5. Recognizing the "Priority Man"

What happens when a man who *is* capable of consistency finally shows up?

For a reclaimed woman, this can actually be quite jarring. Because your brain has been wired for the "chaos of the spark," a healthy, consistent man might initially feel "boring" (Chapter 24). You might feel the urge to self-sabotage or to go back to the "bad boy" who gave you those familiar, painful butterflies.

The Priority Man's Signature:

- **He is Predictable:** You don't have to guess. He says he'll call, and he calls. He says he'll see you Friday, and he shows up on Friday.
- **He is Transparent:** He tells you how he feels. He doesn't play "vague" games to keep you off-balance.
- **He Values Your Voice:** He doesn't want a "Cool Girl"; he wants *you*. He respects your boundaries and is intrigued by your opinions.
- **He is Proactive:** He doesn't wait for you to "manage" the relationship. He is an active participant in building the bridge.

When you find this man, your job is to **allow the safety**. Don't run from the calm. Lean into it. This is what you've been working for.

6. The "Hoover" and the Test of Time

As you move forward, the "Option-Makers" from your past *will* return. We call this **Hoovering**. They will sense your new energy, this vibrant, self-assured frequency, and they will try to "re-option" you. They will send the "I've been thinking about you" text or the "I saw this and thought of you" meme.

The Reclaimed Woman's Response: You do not engage. You do not seek closure. You do not explain your new boundaries. Why? Because **Access is a Privilege**, and they have forfeited theirs.

You don't need to be mean; you just need to be **Indifferent**. Indifference is the ultimate sign of healing. When he no longer has the power to make you angry, he no longer has any power at all.

7. Your Manifesto: The Laws of the Reclaimed Woman

To seal this journey, I want you to read these words aloud. These are not just sentences; they are the new laws of your reality.

> **I am the primary source of my own safety, joy, and validation.**
>
> **I will no longer whisper my needs to avoid someone else's discomfort.**
>
> **I would rather be alone and grounded than "with someone" and anxious.**
>
> **My time is my most precious asset, and I only invest it in people who provide a high return of consistency and respect.**
>
> **I am a "Priority," not an "Option". Anyone who treats me otherwise is simply showing me that they do not belong in my future.**
>
> **I trust my data over my dreams. I trust his actions over his words.**
>
> **I am the architect of a life so beautiful that a partner is an invitation, not a rescue.**

8. Final Words: Walk Toward the Sun

The journey of "Reclaiming the Woman Within" never truly ends; it just gets easier. There will be days when the old "Option" feelings creep back in. There will be days when you feel lonely or when you doubt your worth.

In those moments, I want you to go back to the **Somatic Exercises**. Breathe. Connect with your body. Remember the "Load Tests." And most importantly, remember that you have already done the hardest part: **You decided that you were worth the work.**

You are a woman of depth, intelligence, and immense value. You are a "Priority" because you have chosen to prioritize *yourself.*

Go out into the world with your head high, your boundaries firm, and your heart open—but gated. You are the prize. You are the destination. You are the reclaimed woman.

Now, go live like it.

THE PRIORITY LIFE DAILY CHECKLIST

This is your practical manual for maintaining the internal shift you have achieved. It is not a list of chores; it is a set of operating standards designed to keep your nervous system out of the **Option Cycle** and firmly planted in your own sovereignty. Use this every morning to set your frequency and every evening to audit your data.

The Morning Alignment: Establishing Sovereignty

Goal: To validate yourself before the world, or an external notification, has the chance to do it for you.

- **The Phone-Free First Hour:** Do not check notifications, DMs, or texts for the first 60 minutes of your day. This protects your prefrontal cortex from entering a reactive, "seeking" state before you have centered yourself.
- **The Somatic Grounding:** Spend two minutes doing the **Low-Frequency Hum** (Chapter 18) or a quick jaw release. Remind your body that it is safe, grounded, and in control of its own environment.
- **The Priority Declaration:** Look in the mirror and state your "Creed of Priority." "I am the primary source of my own safety. Today, my peace is non-negotiable."
- **The Solo Win:** Identify one thing you will do today solely for your own joy, not for a digital audience and not for a partner's approval.

The Mid-Day Discernment: The Gatekeeper's Check

Goal: To monitor your performance levels and maintain boundaries in real-time.

- **The Breath Audit:** At noon, check your breathing. Are you in a "High-Beta" state characterized by shallow chest breathing? If so, take three 5-second inhales to reset your autonomic nervous system.

- **The Communication Buffer:** Before responding to any text that feels like a "breadcrumb" or a last-minute request, apply the **24-Hour Buffer** (Chapter 19). Ask: "Am I responding to maintain their interest, or because this adds genuine value to my day?"
- **The Authenticity Check:** In your interactions today, did you swallow a "no" or edit your opinion to be more "palatable"? If yes, consciously correct it in your next interaction.
- **The "Let Them" Pause:** If someone is being inconsistent, quiet, or vague, consciously repeat the mantra: **"Let them."** Do not chase, do not decode, and do not fill the silence.

The Evening Synthesis: Data Over Dreams

Goal: To strip away vague hope and review the raw data of your day.

- **The Load Test Review:** If you conducted a test today (Chapter 25), what was the result? Focus on the **Action**, not the **Explanation**.
    - o *Example:* "He didn't call when he said he would (Action). He was tired (Explanation - ignore this)."
- **The Social Portfolio Audit:** Did you connect with an "Anchor" or a "Joy-Maker" today? (Chapter 20). If you spent more time ruminating on an "Option" than engaging with a reliable support system, reach out to a friend now.
- **The Mastery Minute:** Identify one thing you improved on today. Acknowledge your competence in your career, your hobbies, or your emotional regulation.
- **The Sanctuary Reset:** Clear your physical space. Make your bedroom a "Sovereign Sanctuary" (Chapter 21). Ensure it reflects your comfort and your aesthetic.

The Emergency Protocol

Use this whenever you feel the urge to "self-abandon" or "chase" an inconsistent spark.

1. **Stop the Scroll:** Close the app. Put the phone in another room.
2. **Identify the Trigger:** Is this sensation loneliness, boredom, or a genuine biological need for connection?

3. **The 15-Minute Flow State:** Engage in a high-concentration activity like a puzzle, a workout, or reading to break the dopamine loop.
4. **Phone a Mirror:** Call a person who tells you the truth. Say: "I am feeling the urge to settle for crumbs. Remind me who I am."

The Weekly Priority Audit

Perform this audit every Sunday to ensure you are staying aligned with your new standards.

Question	Yes	No	Required Action
Did I leave my weekend "open" for a maybe?			If yes, book a solo date for next Saturday immediately.
Did I encounter a red flag that I ignored?			If yes, initiate the **Fast Exit** (Chapter 22).
Does my body feel more calm than "excited"?			If yes, celebrate. You are successfully rewiring your nervous system.
Have I been the "project manager" of a connection?			If yes, enter the **Observational Pause** (Chapter 25).

You now have the complete roadmap, the exercises, and the daily maintenance plan. You are no longer navigating by chance; you are navigating by design.

If you enjoyed this book, I'd greatly appreciate a review on Amazon because it helps me to create more books that people want. It would mean a lot to hear from you.

To leave a review:

1. Open your camera app.
2. Point your mobile device at the QR code.
3. The review page will appear in your web browser.

Thanks for your support!

HERE'S ANOTHER BOOK BY SEBASTIAN NOCTURNE THAT YOU MIGHT LIKE

RESOURCES

Introduction

Books

- Bancroft, L. (2002). *Why Does He Do That? Inside the Minds of Angry and Controlling Men*
- Cloud, H., & Townsend, J. (2017). *Boundaries: When to Say Yes, How to Say No to Take Control of Your Life*
- Linehan, M. M. (2014). *DBT Skills Training Handouts and Worksheets*
- Robbins, M. (2025). *The Let Them Theory*
- Van der Kolk, B. (2014). *The Body Keeps the Score: Brain, Mind, and Body in the Healing of Trauma*
- Wood Brooks, A. (2025). *Talk: The Science of Conversation and the Art of Being Ourselves*

Online resources

- https://www.ijsrtjournal.com/article/The-Neurochemistry-of-Heartbreak-Unravelling-the-Complex-Interplay-of-Brain-Regions-Emotions-and-Neurotransmitters-in-Relationship-Breakups
- https://www.mcleanhospital.org/dbt-strategies
- https://therapygroupdc.com/therapist-dc-blog/setting-relationship-boundaries-a-therapist%E2%80%91guided-roadmap/
- https://www.pnas.org/doi/10.1073/pnas.2400022121
- https://animosanopsychiatry.com/blog/neuroplasticity-and-cbt-how-trauma-reshapes-the-brain/
- https://mindfulspark.org/2025/08/25/rising-from-the-ashes-reclaiming-your-life-after-a-toxic-relationship/
- https://www.talktoangel.com/blog/neuroscience-of-heartbreak-why-it-feels-like-physical-pain

Chapter 1

Books

- Bancroft, L. (2002). *Why Does He Do That? Inside the Minds of Angry and Controlling Men.*
- Cloud, H., & Townsend, J. (2017). *Boundaries: When to Say Yes, How to Say No to Take Control of Your Life.*
- Lerner, H. (1985). *The Dance of Anger: A Woman's Guide to Changing the Patterns of Intimate Relationships.*
- Linehan, M. M. (2014). *DBT Skills Training Handouts and Worksheets.*
- Robbins, M. (2025). *The Let Them Theory.*
- Van der Kolk, B. (2014). *The Body Keeps the Score: Brain, Mind, and Body in the Healing of Trauma.*

Online Resources

- https://therapygroupdc.com/therapist-dc-blog/setting-relationship-boundaries-a-therapist%E2%80%91guided-roadmap/
- https://www.talktoangel.com/blog/psychology-of-breadcrumbing-reward-and-intermittent-validation
- https://www.gaslightingcheck.com/blog/intermittent-reinforcement-manipulation
- https://www.pnas.org/doi/10.1073/pnas.2400022121
- https://www.ijsrtjournal.com/article/The-Neurochemistry-of-Heartbreak-Unravelling-the-Complex-Interplay-of-Brain-Regions-Emotions-and-Neurotransmitters-in-Relationship-Breakups
- https://www.mcleanhospital.org/dbt-strategie

Chapter 2

Books

- Fullerton, D.P. (2025). *The Ultra Practical Workbook for Overcoming Avoidant Attachment.*
- Linehan, M. M. (2014). *DBT Skills Training Handouts and Worksheets.*
- Robbins, M. (2025). *The Let Them Theory.*

- Wood Brooks, A. (2025). *Talk: The Science of Conversation and the Art of Being Ourselves.*
- Van der Kolk, B. (2014). *The Body Keeps the Score: Brain, Mind, and Body in the Healing of Trauma.*

Online Resources

- https://medium.com/activated-thinker/2026-relationship-buzzwords-a-dictionary-of-modern-dating-6574b2545550
- https://theotherclinic.sg/2025/02/15/the-psychology-behind-online-dating-why-more-choices-can-lead-to-fewer-connections/
- https://www.talktoangel.com/blog/reminders-for-modern-dating-in-2026
- https://www.gaslightingcheck.com/blog/intermittent-reinforcement-manipulation
- https://www.wearehuman8.com/blog/gen-z-in-2025-navigating-digital-exhaustion-in-a-digitally-native-world/
- https://www.arkhamrise.com/blog/relationship-buzzwords-of-2025-evidence-based-insights-for-2026
- https://www.ijsrtjournal.com/article/The-Neurochemistry-of-Heartbreak-Unravelling-the-Complex-Interplay-of-Brain-Regions-Emotions-and-Neurotransmitters-in-Relationship-Breakups)

Chapter 3

Books

- Fullerton, D.P. (2025). *The Ultra Practical Workbook for Overcoming Avoidant Attachment.*
- Lerner, H. (1985). *The Dance of Anger: A Woman's Guide to Changing the Patterns of Intimate Relationships.*
- Linehan, M. M. (2014). *DBT Skills Training Handouts and Worksheets.*
- Mercurio, Z. (2025). *The Power of Mattering.*
- Robbins, M. (2025). *The Let Them Theory.*
- Van der Kolk, B. (2014). *The Body Keeps the Score: Brain, Mind, and Body in the Healing of Trauma.*

Online Resources

- https://www.pnas.org/doi/10.1073/pnas.2400022121
- https://www.intuiwell.com/personal-growth/external-validation-the-hidden-cycle-that-fuels-anxiety/ *(https://www.researchgate.net/publication/395533166_The_Impact_of_Online_Dating_on_External_Validation_and_Self-Perception)
- https://www.federicoferrarese.co.uk/2026/02/04/reassurance-seeking/
- https://www.talktoangel.com/blog/signs-of-validation-seeking-behaviour-and-ways-to-heal
- https://www.ijsrtjournal.com/article/The-Neurochemistry-of-Heartbreak-Unravelling-the-Complex-Interplay-of-Brain-Regions-Emotions-and-Neurotransmitters-in-Relationship-Breakups

Chapter 4

Books

- Fullerton, D.P. (2025). *The Ultra Practical Workbook for Overcoming Avoidant Attachment.*
- Linehan, M. M. (2014). *DBT Skills Training Handouts and Worksheets.*
- Robbins, M. (2025). *The Let Them Theory.*
- Schwartz, B. (2004). *The Paradox of Choice: Why More Is Less.*
- Wood Brooks, A. (2025). *Talk: The Science of Conversation and the Art of Being Ourselves.*

Online Resources

- https://medium.com/@metbynick/when-dating-becomes-a-second-shift-317dac1b286f
- https://theotherclinic.sg/2025/02/15/the-psychology-behind-online-dating-why-more-choices-can-lead-to-fewer-connections/
- https://mtch.com/single-news/the-human-connection-study-gen-z-believes-in-true-love-more-than-any-other-generation-but-only-55-feel-prepared-for-it/

- https://www.talktoangel.com/blog/dating-app-exhaustion-tips-to-protect-your-mental-health
- https://thepaige.au/burnt-out-from-dating-experts-reveal-how-to-get-back-in-the-game/
- https://www.findarticles.com/kinsey-scientist-rebuts-myths-about-modern-dating/

Reflection Exercises: Chapter 1-4

Books

- Fullerton, D.P. (2025). *The Ultra Practical Workbook for Overcoming Avoidant Attachment.*
- Linehan, M. M. (2014). *DBT Skills Training Handouts and Worksheets.*
- Mercurio, Z. (2025). *The Power of Mattering: How Leaders Can Create a Culture of Significance.*
- Robbins, M. (2025). *The Let Them Theory.*
- Schwartz, B. (2004). *The Paradox of Choice: Why More Is Less.*
- Van der Kolk, B. (2014). *The Body Keeps the Score: Brain, Mind, and Body in the Healing of Trauma.*

Online Resources

- (https://www.ijsrtjournal.com/article/The-Neurochemistry-of-Heartbreak-Unravelling-the-Complex-Interplay-of-Brain-Regions-Emotions-and-Neurotransmitters-in-Relationship-Breakups)
- https://www.mcleanhospital.org/dbt-strategies
- https://therapygroupdc.com/therapist-dc-blog/setting-relationship-boundaries-a-therapist%E2%80%91guided-roadmap/
- https://www.pnas.org/doi/10.1073/pnas.2400022121
- https://mtch.com/single-news/the-human-connection-study-gen-z-believes-in-true-love-more-than-any-other-generation-but-only-55-feel-prepared-for-it/
- https://theotherclinic.sg/2025/02/15/the-psychology-behind-online-dating-why-more-choices-can-lead-to-fewer-connections/

- https://www.talktoangel.com/blog/psychology-of-breadcrumbing-reward-and-intermittent-validation

Chapter 5

Books

- Fullerton, D.P. (2025). *The Ultra Practical Workbook for Overcoming Avoidant Attachment.*
- Lerner, H. (1985). *The Dance of Anger: A Woman's Guide to Changing the Patterns of Intimate Relationships.*
- Robbins, M. (2025). *The Let Them Theory.*
- Rosenthal, M. (2025). *Your Life After Trauma: Powerful Practices to Reclaim Your Identity.*
- Van der Kolk, B. (2014). *The Body Keeps the Score: Brain, Mind, and Body in the Healing of Trauma.*

Online Resources

- https://blog.personaldevelopmentschool.com/post/emotional-unavailability
- https://www.psychologytoday.com/us/blog/social-instincts/202508/why-you-keep-falling-for-emotionally-unavailable-people
- https://drtruitt.com/trauma-is-not-your-story-reclaim-your-identity-after-abuse/
- https://sweetinstitute.com/healing-from-emotional-neglect-understanding-inner-child-wounds-and-reclaiming-emotional-freedom/
- https://www.attachmentproject.com/love/emotional-unavailability/
- https://researchopenworld.com/attachment-and-trauma-in-therapy-a-neuroaffective-developmental-perspective/
- https://www.bhattpsychotherapy.com/post/overcoming-identity-crisis-healing-from-childhood-trauma-given-by-parents
- https://pmc.ncbi.nlm.nih.gov/articles/PMC7594748/

Chapter 6

Books

- Fullerton, D.P. (2025). *The Ultra Practical Workbook for Overcoming Avoidant Attachment.*
- Gottman, J. (2015). *The Seven Principles for Making Marriage Work.*
- Robbins, M. (2025). *The Let Them Theory.*
- Smith, J. (2022). *Why Has Nobody Told Me This Before?.*
- Van der Kolk, B. (2014). *The Body Keeps the Score: Brain, Mind, and Body in the Healing of Trauma.*

Online Resources

- https://www.gottman.com/blog/stonewalling-in-relationships/
- https://theprivatetherapiscritic.co.uk/blog/dismissive-avoidant-attachment/
- https://www.psychologytoday.com/za/blog/happy-singlehood/202212/how-to-know-if-someone-is-emotionally-unavailable
- https://www.attachmentproject.com/love/emotional-unavailability/
- https://www.talktoangel.com/blog/reminders-for-modern-dating-in-2026
- https://www.southdenvertherapy.com/blog/stonewalling-in-relationships
- https://www.ijsrtjournal.com/article/The-Neurochemistry-of-Heartbreak-Unravelling-the-Complex-Interplay-of-Brain-Regions-Emotions-and-Neurotransmitters-in-Relationship-Breakups
- https://counselingcentergroup.com/ending-relationships-dbt-skill/

Chapter 7

Books

- Biringen, Z. (2008). *Emotional Availability: Counseling as an Intervention.*
- Brown, B. (2010). *The Gifts of Imperfection.*

- Cacioppo, J. T., & Patrick, W. (2008). *Loneliness: Human Nature and the Need for Social Connection.*
- Cloud, H., & Townsend, J. (2017). *Boundaries: When to Say Yes, How to Say No.*
- Robbins, M. (2025). *The Let Them Theory.*

Online Resources

- https://loneliness.org.nz/loneliness/science/biology/
- https://isr.umich.edu/news-events/news-releases/the-loneliness-paradox-being-alone-may-not-be-so-bad/
- https://www.psychologytoday.com/za/blog/the-asymmetric-brain/202602/9-key-insights-from-research-about-staying-single
- https://www.talktoangel.com/blog/counselling-for-monophobia-fear-of-being-alone
- https://abbymedcalf.com/why-were-so-afraid-to-be-alone-and-the-five-steps-to-feel-at-ease-with-yourself/
- https://www.resiliencetherapypllc.com/blog/dating-app-burnout-protecting-your-mental-health-in-the-digital-dating-world
- https://councilforrelationships.org/one-two-three-time-a-time-prioritization-strategy-for-adults/

Chapter 8

Books

- Fullerton, D.P. (2025). *The Ultra Practical Workbook for Overcoming Avoidant Attachment.*
- Linehan, M. M. (2014). *DBT Skills Training Handouts and Worksheets.*
- Mercurio, Z. (2025). *The Power of Mattering.*
- Robbins, M. (2025). *The Let Them Theory.*
- Van der Kolk, B. (2014). *The Body Keeps the Score.*
- Wood Brooks, A. (2025). *Talk: The Science of Conversation and the Art of Being Ourselves.*

Online Resources

- https://thedepressionproject.com/blogs/news/journal-prompts-to-help-you-process-trauma
- https://positivepsychology.com/journaling-prompts/
- https://www.ijsrtjournal.com/article/The-Neurochemistry-of-Heartbreak-Unravelling-the-Complex-Interplay-of-Brain-Regions-Emotions-and-Neurotransmitters-in-Relationship-Breakups
- https://drtruitt.com/trauma-is-not-your-story-reclaim-your-identity-after-abuse/
- https://sweetinstitute.com/healing-from-emotional-neglect-understanding-inner-child-wounds-and-reclaiming-emotional-freedom/
- https://www.talktoangel.com/blog/signs-of-validation-seeking-behaviour-and-ways-to-heal
- https://pmc.ncbi.nlm.nih.gov/articles/PMC7594748/
- https://www.pnas.org/doi/10.1073/pnas.2400022121
- https://www.intuiwell.com/personal-growth/external-validation-the-hidden-cycle-that-fuels-anxiety/
- https://www.resiliencetherapypllc.com/blog/dating-app-burnout-protecting-your-mental-health-in-the-digital-dating-world
- https://www.adaptivebehavioralservices.com/mental-wellness-blog/toxic-relationship-recovery-guide-2025
- https://www.researchgate.net/publication/388271830_Coping_with_mobile-online-dating_fatigue_and_the_negative_self-fulfilling_prophecy_of_digital_dating

Reflection Exercises: Chapter 5 to 8

Books

- Beck, J. S. (2011). *Cognitive Behavior Therapy: Basics and Beyond.*
- Fullerton, D.P. (2025). *The Ultra Practical Workbook for Overcoming Avoidant Attachment.*
- Gottman, J. (2015). *The Seven Principles for Making Marriage Work.*

- Linehan, M. M. (2014). *DBT Skills Training Handouts and Worksheets.*
- Mercurio, Z. (2025). *The Power of Mattering: How Leaders Can Create a Culture of Significance.*
- Robbins, M. (2025). *The Let Them Theory.*
- Van der Kolk, B. (2014). *The Body Keeps the Score: Brain, Mind, and Body in the Healing of Trauma.*

Online Resources

- https://positivepsychology.com/journaling-prompts/
- https://dialecticalbehaviortherapy.com/cbt/cognitive-restructuring/
- https://sweetinstitute.com/healing-from-emotional-neglect-understanding-inner-child-wounds-and-reclaiming-emotional-freedom/
- https://www.mcleanhospital.org/dbt-strategies
- https://therapygroupdc.com/therapist-dc-blog/setting-relationship-boundaries-a-therapist-guided-roadmap/
- https://www.talktoangel.com/blog/neuroscience-of-heartbreak-why-it-feels-like-physical-pain
- https://www.psychologytoday.com/us/blog/social-instincts/202508/why-you-keep-falling-for-emotionally-unavailable-people
- https://isr.umich.edu/news-events/news-releases/the-loneliness-paradox-being-alone-may-not-be-so-bad/

Chapter 9

Books

- Bancroft, L. (2002). *Why Does He Do That? Inside the Minds of Angry and Controlling Men*
- Fullerton, D.P. (2025). *The Ultra Practical Workbook for Overcoming Avoidant Attachment*
- Linehan, M. M. (2014). *DBT Skills Training Handouts and Worksheets*
- Robbins, M. (2025). *The Let Them Theory*

- Van der Kolk, B. (2014). *The Body Keeps the Score: Brain, Mind, and Body in the Healing of Trauma*
- Wood Brooks, A. (2025). *Talk: The Science of Conversation and the Art of Being Ourselves*

Online Resources

- https://www.ijsrtjournal.com/article/The-Neurochemistry-of-Heartbreak-Unravelling-the-Complex-Interplay-of-Brain-Regions-Emotions-and-Neurotransmitters-in-Relationship-Breakups
- https://med.stanford.edu/news/insights/2025/03/gut-brain-connection-long-covid-anxiety-parkinsons.html
- https://therapygroupdc.com/therapist-dc-blog/setting-relationship-boundaries-a-therapist%E2%80%91guided-roadmap/
- https://www.psychologytoday.com/us/blog/the-magic-in-the-tragic/202601/why-first-date-jitters-feel-different-in-2026
- https://www.talktoangel.com/blog/neuroscience-of-heartbreak-why-it-feels-like-physical-pain
- https://pmc.ncbi.nlm.nih.gov/articles/PMC12940574/
- https://www.rccs.org.uk/post/the-polyvagal-theory-understanding-the-science-of-safety-and-connection
- https://blogs.bcm.edu/2025/02/14/what-are-considered-relationship-red-flags/

Chapter 10

Books

- Beck, J. S. (2011). *Cognitive Behavior Therapy: Basics and Beyond*
- Biringen, Z. (2008). *Emotional Availability: Counseling as an Intervention*
- Fisher, H. E. (2004). *Why We Love: The Nature and Chemistry of Romantic Love*
- Gottman, J. (2015). *The Seven Principles for Making Marriage Work*
- Linehan, M. M. (2014). *DBT Skills Training Handouts and Worksheets*
- Mercurio, Z. (2025). *The Power of Mattering*

- Robbins, M. (2025). *The Let Them Theory*
- Van der Kolk, B. (2014). *The Body Keeps the Score: Brain, Mind, and Body in the Healing of Trauma*

Online Resources

- https://www.ijsrtjournal.com/article/The-Neurochemistry-of-Heartbreak-Unravelling-the-Complex-Interplay-of-Brain-Regions-Emotions-and-Neurotransmitters-in-Relationship-Breakups
- https://www.endocrine.org/news-and-advocacy/news-room/endo-annual-meeting/endo-2025-press-releases/gonsalvez-press-release
- https://medium.com/@joseph.castroworks/your-brain-on-breakups-why-pain-feels-like-withdrawal-de622cd319af
- https://elifesciences.org/articles/98652
- https://pmc.ncbi.nlm.nih.gov/articles/PMC12907179/
- https://pmc.ncbi.nlm.nih.gov/articles/PMC4826767/
- https://www.talktoangel.com/blog/neuroscience-of-heartbreak-why-it-feels-like-physical-pain
- https://rccaustin.com/blog/2025/3/31/the-effect-of-a-break-up-what-happens-in-your-brain
- https://ahead-app.com/blog/Heartbreak/why-you-feel-so-depressed-after-a-breakup-what-your-brain-needs
- https://pmc.ncbi.nlm.nih.gov/articles/PMC12241886/

Chapter 11

Books

- Beck, J. S. (2011). *Cognitive Behavior Therapy: Basics and Beyond*
- Fullerton, D. P. (2025). *The Ultra Practical Workbook for Overcoming Avoidant Attachment*
- Linehan, M. M. (2014). *DBT Skills Training Handouts and Worksheets*
- Robbins, M. (2025). *The Let Them Theory*
- Van der Kolk, B. (2014). *The Body Keeps the Score: Brain, Mind, and Body in the Healing of Trauma*

- Wood Brooks, A. (2025). *Talk: The Science of Conversation and the Art of Being Ourselves*

Online Resources

- https://www.rccs.org.uk/post/the-polyvagal-theory-understanding-the-science-of-safety-and-connection
- https://pmc.ncbi.nlm.nih.gov/articles/PMC12940574/
- https://www.mcleanhospital.org/dbt-strategies
- https://health.clevelandclinic.org/what-does-the-vagus-nerve-do
- https://www.talktoangel.com/blog/neuroscience-of-heartbreak-why-it-feels-like-physical-pain
- https://pmc.ncbi.nlm.nih.gov/articles/PMC12907179/
- https://resiliencecounselinghtx.com/somatic-therapy-exercises/
- https://www.gentleobservations.com/post/14-practical-somatic-therapy-strategies-for-adults-and-kids

Chapter 12

Books

- Fullerton, D.P. (2025). *The Ultra Practical Workbook for Overcoming Avoidant Attachment*
- Robbins, M. (2025). *The Let Them Theory: A Life-Changing Tool Millions of People Can't Stop Talking About*
- Schwartz, B. (2004). *The Paradox of Choice: Why More Is Less*
- Van der Kolk, B. (2014). *The Body Keeps the Score: Brain, Mind, and Body in the Healing of Trauma*
- Wood Brooks, A. (2025). *Talk: The Science of Conversation and the Art of Being Ourselves*

Online Resources

- https://baptisthealth.net/baptist-health-news/could-a-break-from-your-smartphone-rewire-your-brain-the-science-says-yes
- https://www.homeopathy360.com/a-neurobehavioral-and-holistic-framework-to-digital-detoxing/
- https://pmc.ncbi.nlm.nih.gov/articles/PMC4826767/
- https://www.sciencefocus.com/science/dopamine-detox-focus-mood

- https://newdirectionsbrooklyn.com/dopamine-detox-mental-health-trend-or-meaningful-reset/
- https://thriveworks.com/help-with/self-care/dopamine-detox/
- https://www.hrsolidarity.org/category/blog/
- https://www.intuiwell.com/personal-growth/external-validation-the-hidden-cycle-that-fuels-anxiety/

Reflection Questions: Chapters 9 to 12

Books

- Beck, J. S. (2011). *Cognitive Behavior Therapy: Basics and Beyond*
- Fullerton, D. P. (2025). *The Ultra Practical Workbook for Overcoming Avoidant Attachment*
- Gottman, J. (2015). *The Seven Principles for Making Marriage Work*
- Linehan, M. M. (2014). *DBT Skills Training Handouts and Worksheets*
- Mercurio, Z. (2025). *The Power of Mattering*
- Robbins, M. (2025). *The Let Them Theory*
- Van der Kolk, B. (2014). *The Body Keeps the Score: Brain, Mind, and Body in the Healing of Trauma*

Online Resources

- https://www.rccs.org.uk/post/the-polyvagal-theory-understanding-the-science-of-safety-and-connection
- https://pmc.ncbi.nlm.nih.gov/articles/PMC12907179/
- https://baptisthealth.net/baptist-health-news/could-a-break-from-your-smartphone-rewire-your-brain-the-science-says-yes
- https://medium.com/@joseph.castroworks/your-brain-on-breakups-why-pain-feels-like-withdrawal-de622cd319af
- (https://www.ijsrtjournal.com/article/The-Neurochemistry-of-Heartbreak-Unravelling-the-Complex-Interplay-of-Brain-Regions-Emotions-and-Neurotransmitters-in-Relationship-Breakups)
- https://health.clevelandclinic.org/what-does-the-vagus-nerve-do
- https://resiliencecounselinghtx.com/somatic-therapy-exercises/

- https://www.gentleobservations.com/post/14-practical-somatic-therapy-strategies-for-adults-and-kids

Chapter 13

Books

- Bancroft, L. (2002). *Why Does He Do That? Inside the Minds of Angry and Controlling Men*
- Cloud, H., & Townsend, J. (2017). *Boundaries: When to Say Yes, How to Say No to Take Control of Your Life*
- Evans, P. (2010). *The Verbally Abusive Relationship: How to Recognize It and How to Respond*
- Linehan, M. M. (2014). *DBT Skills Training Handouts and Worksheets*
- Robbins, M. (2025). *The Let Them Theory: A Life-Changing Tool Millions of People Can't Stop Talking About*
- Van der Kolk, B. (2014). *The Body Keeps the Score: Brain, Mind, and Body in the Healing of Trauma*

Online Resources

- https://therapygroupdc.com/therapist-dc-blog/setting-relationship-boundaries-a-therapist%E2%80%91guided-roadmap/
- https://www.mcleanhospital.org/dbt-strategies
- https://www.gottman.com/blog/red-flags-vs-growth-areas-how-to-distinguish-and-navigate-them/
- https://www.psychologytoday.com/us/blog/the-magic-in-the-tragic/202601/why-first-date-jitters-feel-different-in-2026
- https://www.talktoangel.com/blog/reminders-for-modern-dating-in-2026
- https://blogs.bcm.edu/2025/02/14/what-are-considered-relationship-red-flags/
- https://pmc.ncbi.nlm.nih.gov/articles/PMC12940574/

Chapter 14

Books

- Linehan, M. M. (2014). *DBT Skills Training Handouts and Worksheets.*

- Robbins, M. (2025). *The Let Them Theory.*
- Wood Brooks, A. (2025). *Talk: The Science of Conversation and the Art of Being Ourselves.*
- Cloud, H., & Townsend, J. (2017). *Boundaries: When to Say Yes, How to Say No to Take Control of Your Life.*
- Fullerton, D.P. (2025). *The Ultra Practical Workbook for Overcoming Avoidant Attachment.*

Online Resources

- https://www.nature.com/articles/nrn3341
  https://www.mcleanhospital.org/dbt-strategies
  https://www.gottman.com/blog/softening-the-start-up/
- https://medium.com/activated-thinker/2026-relationship-buzzwords
- https://resiliencecounselinghtx.com/somatic-therapy-exercises/

Chapter 15

Books

- Evans, P. (2010). *The Verbally Abusive Relationship: How to Recognize It and How to Respond.*
- Gottman, J., & Silver, N. (2015). *The Seven Principles for Making Marriage Work.*
- Lerner, H. (1985). *The Dance of Anger.*
- Linehan, M. M. (2014). *DBT Skills Training Handouts and Worksheets.*
- Robbins, M. (2025). *The Let Them Theory.*
- Van der Kolk, B. (2014). *The Body Keeps the Score.*

Online Resources

- https://www.gottman.com/blog/the-four-horsemen-recognizing-criticism-contempt-defensiveness-and-stonewalling/
- https://www.mcleanhospital.org/dbt-strategies
- https://www.psychologytoday.com/us/blog/stretching-it/202203/how-spot-the-darvo-tactic
- https://resiliencecounselinghtx.com/somatic-therapy-exercises/

- https://medium.com/activated-thinker/2026-relationship-buzzwords-a-dictionary-of-modern-dating-6574b2545550
- https://www.federicoferrarese.co.uk/2026/02/04/reassurance-seeking/

Chapter 16

Books

- Beattie, M. (1986). *Codependent No More: How to Stop Controlling Others and Start Caring for Yourself.*
- Friel, J., & Friel, L. (1988). *Adult Children: The Secrets of Dysfunctional Families.*
- Gottman, J. (2011). *The Science of Trust: Emotional Attunement for Couples.*
- Heller, A., & Levine, R. (2010). *Attached: The New Science of Adult Attachment.* Lerner, H. (1985). *The Dance of Anger.*
- Robbins, M. (2025). *The Let Them Theory.*

Online Resources

- https://www.apa.org/topics/marriage-relationships/mental-load
- https://www.gottman.com/blog/want-to-improve-your-relationship-start-paying-attention-to-bids/
- https://www.psychologytoday.com/us/blog/fixing-families/201905/the-over-functioner-under-functioner-dynamic
- https://neurosciencenews.com/dopamine-problem-solving-21345/
- https://resiliencecounselinghtx.com/somatic-therapy-exercises/
- https://medium.com/activated-thinker/2026-relationship-buzzwords

Chapter 17

Books

- Braiker, H. B. (2001). *The Disease to Please: Curing the People-Pleasing Syndrome.*
- Cloud, H., & Townsend, J. (2017). *Boundaries: When to Say Yes, How to Say No to Take Control of Your Life.*
- Knight, S. (2016). *The Life-Changing Magic of Not Giving a Fck*.*

- Lerner, H. (1985). *The Dance of Anger.*
- Neff, K. (2011). *Self-Compassion: The Proven Power of Being Kind to Yourself.* Robbins, M. (2025). *The Let Them Theory.*
- Ury, W. (2007). *The Power of a Positive No.*

Online Resources

- https://www.psychologytoday.com/us/blog/conquering-codependency/202101/understanding-the-fawn-response
- https://www.gottman.com/blog/the-courage-to-be-disliked-in-relationships/
- https://www.scientificamerican.com/article/why-social-rejection-hurts-physical-pain/
- https://hbr.org/2018/07/stop-being-so-nice
- https://www.verywellmind.com/fawning-and-trauma-responses-5211015
- https://www.forbes.com/sites/digital-wellness-trends-2026/

Reflection Exercises: Chapters 13 to 17

Books

- Bancroft, L. (2002). *Why Does He Do That? Inside the Minds of Angry and Controlling Men.*
- Cloud, H., & Townsend, J. (2017). *Boundaries: When to Say Yes, How to Say No to Take Control of Your Life.*
- Evans, P. (2010). *The Verbally Abusive Relationship: How to Recognize It and How to Respond.*
- Linehan, M. M. (2014). *DBT Skills Training Handouts and Worksheets.*
- Robbins, M. (2025). *The Let Them Theory: A Life-Changing Tool Millions of People Can't Stop Talking About.*
- Van der Kolk, B. (2014). *The Body Keeps the Score: Brain, Mind, and Body in the Healing of Trauma.*

Online Resources

- https://www.gottman.com/blog/red-flags-vs-growth-areas-how-to-distinguish-them/
- https://www.mcleanhospital.org/dbt-strategies

- https://therapygroupdc.com/therapist-dc-blog/setting-relationship-boundaries-a-therapist-guided-roadmap/
- https://www.psychologytoday.com/us/blog/the-science-connection
- https://health.clevelandclinic.org/what-does-the-vagus-nerve-do

Chapter 18

Books

- Bancroft, L. (2002). *Why Does He Do That? Inside the Minds of Angry and Controlling Men.*
- Linehan, M. M. (2014). *DBT Skills Training Handouts and Worksheets.*
- Matias, M. (2016). *Evolutionary Perspectives on Emotional Suppression in Stratified Societies.*
- Robbins, M. (2025). *The Let Them Theory: A Life-Changing Tool Millions of People Can't Stop Talking About.*
- Van der Kolk, B. (2014). *The Body Keeps the Score.*

Online Resources

- https://www.thelondoncentre.co.uk/treatment-read-more/assertiveness-and-dbt
- https://myyogateacher.com/articles/throat-chakra-vishuddha-guide
- https://www.psychologytoday.com/za/blog/social-instincts/202511/2-ways-to-shield-your-relationship-from-the-silent-treatment
- https://www.talktoangel.com/blog/finding-the-way-out-of-silent-treatment

Chapter 19

Books

- Heller, A., & Levine, R. (2010). *Attached: The New Science of Adult Attachment.*
- Robbins, M. (2025). *The Let Them Theory.*
- Stosny, S. (2008). *How to Improve Your Marriage Without Talking About It.*

- Van der Kolk, B. (2014). *The Body Keeps the Score.*
- Beattie, M. (1986). *Codependent No More.*

Online Resources

- https://www.gottman.com/blog/the-one-thing-that-predicts-divorce/
- https://www.psychologytoday.com/us/blog/the-science-luck/201205/the-psychology-waiting-in-lines
- https://www.healthline.com/health/mental-health/intermittent-reinforcement
- https://www.mcleanhospital.org/essential/anxiety
- https://health.clevelandclinic.org/what-does-the-vagus-nerve-do

Chapter 20

Books

- Brown, B. (2012). *Daring Greatly: How the Courage to Be Vulnerable Transforms the Way We Live, Love, Parent, and Lead.*
- Gottman, J., & Gottman, J. S. (2015). *The Seven Principles for Making Marriage Work.*
- Levine, A., & Heller, R. (2010). *Attached: The New Science of Adult Attachment.*
- Porges, S. W. (2017). *The Pocket Guide to the Polyvagal Theory: The Transformative Power of Feeling Safe.*
- Van der Kolk, B. (2014). *The Body Keeps the Score.*

Online Resources

- https://www.gottman.com/blog/the-importance-of-social-support/
- https://www.helpguide.org/articles/relationships-communication/social-support-for-stress-relief.htm
- https://www.psychologytoday.com/us/basics/oxytocin
- https://www.mcleanhospital.org/essential/shame

Chapter 21

Books

- Maitland, S. (2008). *A Book of Silence.*
- Maslow, A. H. (1943). *A Theory of Human Motivation.*

- Robbins, M. (2025). *The Let Them Theory.*
- Strayed, C. (2012). *Wild: From Lost to Found on the Pacific Crest Trail.*
- Solomon, A. (2017). *The Noonday Demon: An Atlas of Depression.*

Online Resources

- https://www.theschooloflife.com/article/the-art-of-solitude/
- https://www.psychologytoday.com/us/blog/high-octane-women/201201/the-importance-solitude
- https://www.gottman.com/blog/self-care-is-not-selfish/
- https://www.mindful.org/the-science-of-flow/
- https://my.clevelandclinic.org/health/body/23040-endorphins

Reflection Exercises: Chapters 18 to 21

Books

- Linehan, M. M. (2014). *DBT Skills Training Handouts and Worksheets.*
- Porges, S. W. (2017). *The Pocket Guide to the Polyvagal Theory.*
- Robbins, M. (2025). *The Let Them Theory.*
- Van der Kolk, B. (2014). *The Body Keeps the Score.*

Online Resources

- https://www.gottman.com/blog/the-silent-treatment/
- https://www.mcleanhospital.org/dbt-strategies
- https://www.psychologytoday.com/us/basics/flow

Chapter 22

Books

- Cloud, H. (2011). *Necessary Endings.*
- Levine, A., & Heller, R. (2010). *Attached.*
- Porges, S. (2011). *The Polyvagal Theory.*
- Stern, R. (2018). *The Gaslight Effect.*

Online Resources

- https://www.gottman.com/blog/6-early-warning-signs-of-a-troubled-relationship/

- https://www.psychologytoday.com/us/blog/the-right-mindset/202005/the-science-behind-gut-feelings
- https://www.healthline.com/health/love-bombing

Chapter 23

Core Literature

- Brown, B. (2012). *Daring Greatly.*
- Cain, S. (2012). *Quiet.*
- Gottman, J. (2011). *The Science of Trust.*
- Lerner, H. (1985). *The Dance of Anger.*

Online Resources

- https://www.psychologytoday.com/us/blog/the-high-stakes-dating/202104/the-trap-of-impression-management-in-dating
- https://www.ted.com/talks/brene_brown_the_power_of_vulnerability
- https://www.theschooloflife.com/article/how-to-be-yourself/

Chapter 24

Book

- Gottman, J. (2011). *The Science of Trust.*
- Levine, A., & Heller, R. (2010). *Attached.*
- Hendrix, H. (1988). *Getting the Love You Want.*
- Stan Tatkin (2012). *Wired for Love.*
- Online Resources
- https://www.gottman.com/blog/sliding-door-moments/
- https://www.psychologytoday.com/us/blog/the-high-stakes-dating/202102/why-the-spark-is-bad-way-choose-partner
- https://www.healthline.com/health/relationships/chemistry-vs-compatibility

Chapter 25

Books

- Cloud, H. (2011). *Necessary Endings.*
- Levine, A., & Heller, R. (2010). *Attached.*
- Gottman, J. (2011). *The Science of Trust.*

- Gilbert, D. (2006). *Stumbling on Happiness.*

Online Resources

- https://www.gottman.com/blog/want-to-improve-your-relationship-start-paying-more-attention-to-bids/
- https://www.psychologytoday.com/us/blog/the-high-stakes-dating/202103/why-dating-for-potential-is-dangerous

Reflection Exercises: Chapters 22 to 25

Books

- Cloud, H. (2011). *Necessary Endings.*
- Levine, A., & Heller, R. (2010). *Attached.*
- Gottman, J. (2011). *The Science of Trust.*
- Porges, S. (2017). *The Pocket Guide to Polyvagal Theory.*
- Stern, R. (2018). *The Gaslight Effect.*

Online Resources

- https://www.gottman.com/blog/6-early-warning-signs-of-a-troubled-relationship/
- https://www.psychologytoday.com/us/blog/the-high-stakes-dating/202102/why-the-spark-is-bad-way-choose-partner
- https://www.healthline.com/health/relationships/how-to-set-boundaries
- https://www.mindful.org/a-somatic-practice-to-soothe-your-nervous-system/

Conclusion

Books

- Bancroft, L. (2002). *Why Does He Do That? Inside the Minds of Angry and Controlling Men.*
- Cloud, H., & Townsend, J. (2017). *Boundaries: When to Say Yes, How to Say No to Take Control of Your Life.*
- Gottman, J., & Silver, N. (2015). *The Seven Principles for Making Marriage Work.*
- Levine, A., & Heller, R. (2010). *Attached.*
- Porges, S. (2017). *The Pocket Guide to the Polyvagal Theory.*
- Robbins, M. (2025). *The Let Them Theory.*

- Van der Kolk, B. (2014). *The Body Keeps the Score.*

Online Resources

- https://www.gottman.com/product/relationship-adviser/
- https://self-compassion.org/category/exercises/
- https://health.clevelandclinic.org/vagus-nerve-stimulation/

www.ingramcontent.com/pod-product-compliance
Lightning Source LLC
LaVergne TN
LVHW010648110826
845149LV00014B/2994
9781968553739